Lay Eucharistic Preaching in a Synodal Catholic Church

Edited by

Gregory Heille, OP

LITURGICAL PRESS
Collegeville, Minnesota

litpress.org

Cover design by Emma Elzinga. Cover art courtesy of Freepik.

Library of Congress Cataloging-in-Publication Data

Names: Heille, Gregory, 1947– editor.
Title: Lay eucharistic preaching in a synodal Catholic Church / edited by Gregory Heille, OP.
Description: Collegeville, Minnesota : Liturgical Press, [2025] | Includes bibliographical references. | Summary: "Twenty-seven preachers and theologians from around the world met in March 2024 for a symposium on the pastoral charge for lay eucharistic preaching. Lay Eucharistic Preaching in a Synodal Catholic Church exemplifies the recommendations proposed at the gathering to lend support and breathe life into the assembly's experience of the homily at Mass"— Provided by publisher.
Identifiers: LCCN 2024055976 (print) | LCCN 2024055977 (ebook) | ISBN 9798400802089 (trade paperback) | ISBN 9798400802096 (epub) | ISBN 9798400802270 (pdf)
Subjects: LCSH: Lay preaching | Catholic preaching. | Lord's Supper—Catholic Church.
Classification: LCC BV4235.L3 L384 2025 (print) | LCC BV4235.L3 (ebook) | DDC 251.0088/282—dc23/eng/20250108
LC record available at https://lccn.loc.gov/2024055976
LC ebook record available at https://lccn.loc.gov/2024055977

Contents

Synodal Church

Participant Essays

Won't You Be My Neighbor?

Sara Fairbanks

The road to St. Patrick's Cathedral in Auckland, New Zealand, was lined with pink shoes to protest the painful discrimination women experience at the hands of the Catholic Church. The women organizing the protest timed the event during Women's Suffrage Day. In 1893, New Zealand was the first country where women won the right to vote!

JoAnn Ayers, one of the organizers, said, "It's women's suffrage anniversary and we're saying through our event that even though women can run New Zealand—we've had women as prime minister, governor general, and chief justice—in the church we're second class and we're saying to the church it's time for change."[1] While today a small percentage of called, gifted, and theologically trained women do various forms of liturgical preaching, the sight of women preaching the Gospel when most of the faithful gather for Sunday worship is still extremely

1. Peter Kirkwood, "New Zealand Catholic Women Display 'Pink Shoes' to Call for Equality in the Church," *National Catholic Reporter*, September 26, 2022, https://www.ncronline.org/news/new-zealand-catholic-women-display-pink-shoes-call-equality-church.

rare, especially with the pushback against the Second Vatican Council. While laymen can take the diaconal road to the pulpit, women are left in the ditch, half-dead. Like the priest and the Levite, many of the church's clergy pass us by, blind and indifferent to our plight.

Many women preachers excluded from the Sunday pulpit experience heart-wrenching rejection. They are stripped of their baptismal identity as "other Christs," equal partners with Christ in the preaching ministry. As a result, the community gathered for Sunday worship rarely experiences the unique ways that the risen Jesus continues to proclaim the Gospel through the voice and lives of women he so values.

The long-held liturgical tradition signifying that Catholic women lack the capacity, right, and duty to preach at the Sunday Eucharist attacks the dignity of women as created in the image of God. Women in the pews are robbed of the opportunity to hear the gospel preached in their own language, interpreted from women's perspectives and life experiences. Until we frequently see and listen to women preach from the pulpit, we will never say, as I once did many years ago, "Wow, I didn't realize women had the spiritual gifts and capacity to preach with such power and conviction."

Jesus asks us, "Who was a neighbor to the robbers' victim?" The true jolt of Jesus' parable is that the enemy Samaritan turns out to be the good neighbor. The Sunday Eucharist need not be a battleground in a war between the sexes. It's about baptismal call, not competition. Women liturgical preachers are a gift of the Holy Spirit, a fire in the church that enkindles faith. These women, called by the living Christ who dwells within them, have the right and duty to serve in collaboration with their brothers as equal partners in the church's mission of liturgical preaching at the Eucharist.

Promoting synodality, Pope Francis loves to image the church as the Good Samaritan who responds in solidarity to those who are poor and on the margins. Mary's prophetic *Magnificat* resounds as the mighty are brought low and the lowly raised through roundtable discussions, deliberations, and voting. Mary Magdalene's "I have seen the Lord!" is heard with believing ears from her brothers. The church as the Good Samaritan echoes the voice of Jesus, who beckons women, "Ask, and it will be given you; search, and you will find; knock, and the door will be opened for you" (Matt 7:7)—that is to say, "You are important to me, and I will hear your voice. Your words will not return to me empty."

As a church of the Good Samaritan, we must never demonize our brothers and sisters but lovingly stand our ground and learn to listen and speak the truth. With God's grace, our secret hearts will risk giving voice to our dream that women and men will one day exercise an equal partnership in the church's preaching mission. We ask our church: Where do you stand? Will you pass women by, or will you lift them up? Brothers and sisters, won't you be my neighbor?[2]

2. These welcoming remarks to participants at our symposium on "The Pastoral Charge for Lay Catholic Eucharistic Preaching" were preached at Night Prayer at Aquinas Institute of Theology on March 12, 2024. The symposium also received preachings by Kayla August, Megan McElroy, Megan Effron, Wayne Cavalier, and Kerstin-Marie Berretz.

A Synodal Path Forward

Gregory Heille

> There is no longer Jew or Greek,
> there is no longer slave or free,
> there is no longer male and female;
> for all of you are one in Christ Jesus.
> —Galatians 3:28

When it comes to laywomen or laymen preaching the homily at Catholic Mass, notwithstanding the canonical prohibition of this practice, the question "Won't you be my neighbor?" invites a synodal reexamination in light of the church's theology and practice of baptism, Eucharist, and ministry.

In December 2022, eight lay ecclesial ministers currently studying or having graduated from Aquinas Institute of Theology's doctor of ministry in preaching asked their faculty to more intentionally give theological backing to their preaching ministry, lest they be all dressed up for the preaching ministry but have no place to go to exercise their calling. In March 2024, we responded to this petition with a synodal symposium on "The Pastoral Charge for Lay Catholic Eucharistic Preaching." The twenty-seven preachers and theologians participating in this symposium submitted a formal petition to the Synod on Synodality for its second session in Rome in October 2024, and we were delighted to see the fruits of our labor in the following mention of lay preaching at the Eucharist in the *Instrumentum Laboris* for the second session: "Many of the demands expressed above also apply to laymen, whose lack of participation in the life of the Church is often lamented. In general, reflection on the role of women often highlights the desire to strengthen all the ministries exercised by the laity (men and women). *There is also a call for adequately trained lay men and women to contribute to preaching the Word of God, including during the celebration of the Eucharist.*"[1]

This book presents the talks and responses from the symposium, the symposium petition to the Synod on Synodality, and several academic and personal essays on the topic. The last book of this nature was *Preaching and the Non-Ordained: An Interdisciplinary Study*, edited by Nadine Foley, OP, published by Liturgical Press in 1983, and based on a conference held by the Dominican Leadership Conference in Columbus, Ohio, in 1982. You can find the opening remarks from that volume reproduced at the end of this book.

For many reasons, an ecclesial conversation about lay preaching in the Catholic Church, and particularly at the Eucharist, has fallen silent for many years. In this synodal moment, many preachers and theologians think it is time to reopen the conversation on this vexing topic.

1. XVI Ordinary General Assembly of the Synod of Bishops, *Instrumentum Laboris* for the Second Session, "*How* to Be a Missionary Synodal Church" (October 2024), under "Foundations," in a section titled "Brothers and Sisters in Christ: A Renewed Reciprocity," 18; emphasis added.

Canonical Background

While the Roman Catholic 1917 Code of Canon Law forbade preaching by the laity (c. 1342 §2[2]), the 1983 Code of Canon Law, following the Second Vatican Council's theology of the laity, acknowledged the possibility of lay preaching by associating the call to preach the Gospel with baptism (c. 759) and stating circumstances where it may be necessary or advantageous for laypersons to preach in a church or oratory (c. 766), while explicitly reserving the eucharistic homily to a priest or deacon (c. 767 §1). The pastor is to observe these canons conscientiously (c. 767 §4), and the norms of the bishop are also to be followed (c. 772 §1).

In May 1987, the Pontifical Commission for the Authentic Interpretation of the Code of Canon Law issued a complementary norm concerning canon 767 §1: "Preaching by lay faithful may not take place within the celebration of the Eucharist at the moment reserved for the homily."[3]

In November 1988, the United States National Conference of Catholic Bishops drafted guidelines based on their interpretation of canon law.[4] These guidelines stated: "The Code of Canon Law places two restrictions, which are fundamental to these guidelines: The preaching of a homily during the Eucharist is strictly reserved to the ordained, and preaching by lay persons, when it occurs in a

2. "All laymen, religious as well, are forbidden to preach in church."

3. "USCCB Decree Implementing Canon 766 of the Code of Canon Law," USCCB Committee on the Liturgy Newsletter XXXVII (December 13, 2001): 49–50.

4. United States Conference of Catholic Bishops, "Guidelines for Lay Preaching," National Catholic News Service, *Origins* 18, no. 25 (1988): 402–4.

church or oratory, requires authorization by the diocesan bishop." Later, the bishops repeated: "Laity or religious should not speak at the time designated for the homily lest the impression be given that the person is giving the homily in the strict sense."[5] Though approved by the bishops, the Vatican Congregation on the Clergy rejected these guidelines because "guidelines" are not binding. Eleven years later, in November 1999, the plenary meeting of the United States Conference of Catholic Bishops approved the "Decree Implementing Canon 766 of the Code of Canon Law," which took effect for all dioceses in the United States in January 2002 and was posted on the USCCB website. In this decree, the bishops state: "The lay faithful who are to be admitted to preach in a church or oratory must be orthodox in faith, and well-qualified, both by the witness of their lives as Christians and by a preparation for preaching appropriate to the circumstances." In alignment with the 1987 complimentary norm mentioned above, the USCCB statement also says: "In providing for preaching by the lay faithful the diocesan bishop may never dispense from the norm which reserves the homily to the sacred ministers."[6]

The *General Instruction of the Roman Missal* issued in March 2003 complies with these laws and norms: "The Homily should ordinarily be given by the Priest Celebrant himself or be entrusted by him to a concelebrating Priest, or from time to time and, if appropriate, to the Deacon, but never to a lay person" (66).[7]

5. USCCB, "Guidelines for Lay Preaching," 403.

6. "USCCB Decree Implementing Canon 766," 49.

7. *General Instruction of the Roman Missal*, approved by the USCCB, November 12, 2002, and confirmed by decree of the Congregation for Divine Worship and the Discipline of the Sacraments,

In March 2004, the Catholic Church's Congregation for Divine Worship and the Discipline of the Sacraments issued *Redemptionis Sacramentum* ("Instruction on Certain Matters to Be Observed or to Be Avoided Regarding the Most Holy Eucharist"), which stated:

> The homily on account of its importance and its nature is reserved to the Priest or Deacon during Mass. As regards other forms of preaching, if necessity demands it in particular circumstances, or if usefulness suggests it in special cases, lay members of Christ's faithful may be allowed to preach in a church or in an oratory outside Mass in accordance with the norm of law. This may be done only on account of a scarcity of sacred ministers in certain places, in order to meet the need, and it may not be transformed from an exceptional measure into an ordinary practice, nor may it be understood as an authentic form of the advancement of the laity. All must remember besides that the faculty for giving such permission belongs to the local Ordinary, and this as regards individual instances; this permission is not the competence of anyone else, even if they are Priests or Deacons.[8]

While the church expressly forbids lay preaching in the place reserved for the homily at the Eucharist, perhaps we should admit that lay preachers frequently

---

March 17, 2003. A footnote to GIRM 66 refers to the Pontifical Commission for the Authentic Interpretation of the *Code of Canon Law*, 1987 response to *dubium* regarding c. 767 §1.

8. Congregation for Divine Worship and the Discipline of the Sacraments, *Redemptionis Sacramentum,* "Instruction on Certain Matters to Be Observed or to Be Avoided Regarding the Most Holy Eucharist" (March 25, 2004) 161.

preach at the time reserved for the homily. In local instances, pastoral leaders make a quiet decision that, in their circumstances, it is necessary or certainly advantageous for a layperson to preach the homily. In today's climate of missionary discipleship and more widespread theological and ministerial formation, many laypeople are motivated and qualified to preach at Mass. Should the church forbid them to do so, or could the church create well-regulated pathways for lay preaching of the homily at Mass when it is advantageous or necessary? What might the eucharistic pulpit look like in a synodal church aspiring to live according to a vision of the people of God, as articulated by the bishops at the Second Vatican Council?

Issues Addressed by the Symposium in St. Louis

As mentioned earlier, in March 2024, five months after the first session of the Synod on Synodality in Rome in October 2023, twenty-seven theologians and preachers from North America, Europe, and Asia met at Aquinas Institute of Theology with these questions in mind. We asked the participants to reflect on the following problem: "Canon law permits lay preaching but restricts lay ecclesial ministers from preaching the homily at Mass. Many theologically trained lay ecclesial ministers have received preaching formation but do not receive an ecclesial commission to preach. Can a theological case be made for the church to charge or commission a more extensive and diverse pool of qualified lay preachers and evangelists to preach the Word of God at the Eucharist?"

The steering committee proposed the following tentative listing of issues for renewed discussion, research, and exploration as participants prepared for the event.

Canonical Issues

Canon law has clarified that the people have a right to hear the Word of God and that bishops are responsible for seeing that the Word is preached. Canon law does not restrict preaching by the laity outside churches and oratories. Canon 766 admits that laypeople may preach in a church or oratory when "necessity requires it in certain circumstances or it seems advantageous in particular cases," thus allowing for a wide range of lay preaching at Word services, Morning and Evening Prayer, etc. However, the preaching of the eucharistic homily remains reserved for ordained clergy. Additional legislation on lay preaching is the prerogative of the national conferences of bishops.

Some canonists suggest that there ought to be a distinction maintained between the power of jurisdiction and the power of orders as this pertains to the authority to preach. The power of jurisdiction is associated with canonical mission, which seems to extend beyond the clerical state. Canon 129 §2 states, "Lay members of the Christian faithful can cooperate in the exercise of this same power according to the norm of law." This canon about the power of jurisdiction could be used to defend the possibility of charging laypeople to preach at the Eucharist.

Pastoral Issues

The people of God have a right to hear the Word of God preached in a way that is consonant with their experience. Sometimes, a layperson can do this. Some canonically permissible but limiting examples include preaching to children and preaching to people in a language not known by the priest. For the most part, however, women and men rarely, if ever, have the chance to hear the Word preached out of women's experience as women.

On the one hand, if preaching is a charism given for the good of the church, it should be exercised by those who have the gift. On the other hand, there ought to be a connection between leadership in the church and preaching. In many parishes, a layperson who knows the community well, often a woman, serves as pastoral leader with responsibility for the faith formation of the community. When this pastoral leader has received the requisite theological education and pastoral formation for preaching, could they have authority as an "ordinary minister" to preach the Word at the Eucharist to the people?

Theological Issues

In discussions about the authority to preach at the Eucharist, there is tension between preserving the identity of the ordained minister and meeting the needs of the people of God. Both values need to be respected if the dialogue is to be effective.

The theological foundation for lay preaching lies in the charism given to all the baptized for ministry and mission. There are diverse ecclesiological interpretations regarding the authorization to preach at the Eucharist. In an ecclesiology where the bishops have the exclusive exercise of the teaching office in the church, it would seem that ordination is required of all who participate in the bishops' faculty to preach. Vatican II, however, has presented us with strands of a different ecclesiology, as seen in some canons in the 1983 Code of Canon Law, in which laypersons share in Christ's priestly, prophetic, and kingly office by their baptism.

No exceptions would ever apply if preaching at Eucharist was "absolutely intrinsic" to ordination. However, exceptions have been made. In addition to those stated above related to the needs of children and language differences, the German bishops allowed lay preaching from 1973 to 1981, with Rome's approval. However, this approval has since been withdrawn.

Liturgical Issues

Those who propose a very restricted understanding identify four essential elements when defining the homily: reflection on the Word of God or another liturgical text, proclaimed by an ordained minister, after the gospel, at the eucharistic liturgy. The argument for offering exceptions to this restriction goes something like this: if a homily is the preaching of an ordained minister proclaimed after the gospel at Eucharist, then the preaching of a layperson at Eucharist cannot be called a homily but is more appropriately given a different name—for example, "reflection on the Scriptures," "lectionary-based liturgical preaching," or simply "preaching." This admittedly nominalist approach to the homily is not very persuasive for some.

Another way of looking at the homily is by examining its purpose. Suppose the purpose is primarily teaching or instruction. Then, it seems logical to reserve the homily to the theological expert, who, until recent times, was unquestionably the ordained priest. In *Fulfilled in Your Hearing: The Homily in the Sunday Assembly* (1982), a more nuanced understanding of the purpose of the homily was proposed by the American bishops: that of "a scriptural interpretation of human existence which enables a community to recognize God's active presence, to respond to that presence in faith through liturgical word and gesture, and beyond the liturgical assembly, through a life lived in conformity with the Gospel."[9] In this understanding of homily as an "interpretative act" the preacher must understand the diverse experiences of the assembly to "interpret the human situation through the Scriptures."[10] This understanding allows for and, some would say, demands a greater diversity of preachers than ordained males.

By generally agreed liturgical principle, the Liturgy of the Word and the Liturgy of the Eucharist form an essential unity. As a manifestation of that unity, ordinarily, the one who presides at the Eucharist ought to preach. This practice cannot, however, be considered an absolute since liturgical law allows a priest other than the presider or even a deacon to preach at the Eucharist. Might qualified laity also be considered "extraordinary ministers of preaching" at the Eucharist, with a canonical mission to preach much as the ordained receive faculties to preach?

9. Bishops' Committee on Priestly Life and Ministry, *Fulfilled in Your Hearing: The Homily in the Sunday Assembly* (Washington, DC: USCCB Publishing, 1982), 29.

10. Bishops' Committee on Priestly Life and Ministry, *Fulfilled in Your Hearing*, 20.

Toward a Common Statement on Lay Preaching in the Eucharist

Ann Garrido

Preparing for the March 2024 Symposium

The *Instrumentum Laboris* issued in June 2023 in preparation for the first general assembly of the Synod on Synodality harvested insights gleaned from earlier listening sessions around the globe to put forward three sets of worksheets pertaining to each of the three key themes of the synod: communion, co-responsibility in mission, and participation. Each set of worksheets posed questions for discernment that it asked members of the synod and members of the church at large to pray and reflect upon.[1] The *Instrumentum Laboris* acknowledged that no one person or group could reflect on all the questions. Still, they invited discerners to pay attention to the

1. *Instrumentum Laboris* for the First Session of the XVI Ordinary General Assembly of the Synod of Bishops (June 2023), 24: "They are 'to be done' not 'to be read' in the sense that they offer an outline for prayer and personal reflection for group and plenary discussion. Similarly, they can be used for in-depth thematic meetings in a synodal style at all levels of Church life."

questions that most spoke to their context, as "this will be their contribution to the common task."[2]

Among the many topics for reflection posed, two in particular spoke to members of the steering committee at Aquinas Institute of Theology as they began planning the March 2024 symposium: (1) "How should we celebrate Baptism, Confirmation and the Eucharist so that they are occasions for witnessing and promoting the participation and co-responsibility of all as active subjects in the life and mission of the Church? How can we renew an understanding of ministry not limited to ordained Ministry alone?" and (2) "How can we discern the baptismal Ministries necessary for mission in a local Church, whether instituted or not? What spaces are available for experimentation at the local level? What value should be attributed to these Ministries? Under what conditions can they be received and recognized by the entire Church?"[3]

Wishing to frame its March 2024 gathering within the larger discernment of the synod, the steering committee at Aquinas Institute of Theology focused on the possibility of lay eucharistic preaching within a synodal church. They invited ecclesiologist Edward Hahnenberg and liturgical theologian Layla Karst to consider lay preaching at the Eucharist anew in light of the synod's work. Could a sound theological argument be made to support expanding the preaching ministry within the Eucharist?

2. *Instrumentum Laboris*, 24. "Some insights will prove particularly stimulating in certain regions of the world, others in different regions. Each person is invited to choose the ones that they feel best enable the richest of their own Church context to be shared with others. This will be their contribution to the common task."

3. *Instrumentum Laboris*, 40 (Section B2.2, Suggestions for Prayer and Preparatory Reflection).

The committee also began to identify potential participants for a symposium on this topic. The list included international representatives from various branches of the Dominican family and scholars and preachers from across the United States, including younger scholars and preachers who had not been part of earlier conversations on this topic in the 1980s and '90s.

The synod's October 2023 synthesis report, "A Synodal Church in Mission," included a proposal to embrace "a wider revision of the Code of Canon Law."[4] The synod also remarked on the possibility of expanding the responsibilities of the instituted ministry of the lector: "This could become a fuller ministry of the Word of God which, in appropriate contexts, could also include preaching."[5]

"A Synodal Church in Mission" also reemphasized the value of ongoing "conversation in the Spirit,"[6] leading symposium invitees to look at the general secretariat of the synod's call to continue local conversations in the Spirit, especially during Lent 2024, as a way to contribute to the preparation of the *Instrumentum Laboris* for the second general assembly of the synod to take place in October 2024.[7] Symposium invitees began to

4. XVI Ordinary General Assembly of the Synod of Bishops, Synthesis Report for the First Session, "A Synodal Church in Mission" (Vatican City: October 4–29, 2023), 7, Theme 1, Proposal R.

5. XVI Ordinary General Assembly, "Synodal Church in Mission," 19, Theme 8, Proposal N.

6. XVI Ordinary General Assembly, "Synodal Church in Mission," 7, Theme 2, Convergences D. For description of the process itself, see the *Instrumentum Laboris* for the first general assembly of the synod, 16.

7. General Secretariat of the Synod, XVI Ordinary General Assembly of the Synod of Bishops, "Towards October 2024" (December 11, 2023), esp. 3–4.

reimagine what might be the outcome of their gathering. Was it possible to shift from an academic model of a symposium focused on crafting a statement primarily intended for the academy to a more synodal model focused on group reflection around the possibilities raised by "A Synodal Church in Mission"? Could we craft a communal statement that we could offer in service to the synod's ongoing discernment around the ministry of preaching?

When considering a synodal approach to the symposium, the steering committee chose to follow each keynote presentation not with an academic *disputatio* of the ideas presented but with a process modeled on conversation in the Spirit. The process would be grounded in prayer and focus on listening for the Holy Spirit moving among us.

During the March 2024 Symposium

After over six months of planning, symposium participants gathered at Aquinas Institute of Theology in St. Louis, Missouri, on March 11–14, 2024. Twenty-four of the invited participants could be present in person; three members critical to the symposium participated from a distance.

On the evening of March 11, participants got to know one another and reviewed the synod's work, especially as it might intersect with the topic of lay eucharistic preaching. The symposium's two facilitators then introduced the conversation in the Spirit process that would follow each set of theological presentations. Each conversation in the Spirit period would begin with the *Adsumus Sancte Spiritus* prayer that guided the synod and would typically involve three rounds of listening in small table groups. The process included time to share one's perspective, what was heard from others' perspectives, and one's sense of the Spirit's movement in the conversation. Silence punctuated each round of sharing. Each conversation group took notes and posted highlights of its discussion on the wall.

The facilitators asked for a group commitment to observe the Chatham House Rule observed by members of the synod assembly. First associated with the Royal Institute of International Affairs in London, the Chatham House Rule sets as a norm that persons attending a meeting might speak freely about information learned at a gathering but cannot attribute a comment to any particular person in the room nor any of their identity markers such as gender, school affiliation, or political party.

While participants shared a great deal of goodwill and like-mindedness about lay preaching at the Eucharist, the facilitators noted that there were likely differences in the group regarding the strength of various theological arguments for or against and the relative importance of the topic in the contemporary Church. As at the synod, such differences did not need to be resolved at the symposium. Following the same three-part outline utilized in "A Synodal Church in Mission," the group listened for convergences. We also listened for differences or matters for consideration. While we anticipated we might arrive at a few proposals to share with the synod, we committed ourselves to letting the Spirit lead the way.

The substantive work of the symposium took place on March 12 and 13. Edward Hahnenberg gave a paper on the theology of ministry on the first morning, and Layla Karst gave a paper on the theology of synodality on the second morning. Two formal responses and a small group conversation in the Spirit followed each paper. Over the two days, each participant was assigned to one of the four afternoon panels to share insight from each person's area of expertise and experience on the topic. Following each panel, participants again broke into small groups to engage in a second variation of the conversation in the Spirit process.

By the late afternoon of the second day, highlights from each of the six conversations in the Spirit were written on newsprint and displayed. Because we observed the Chatham House Rule and no one's name was on the notes, what surfaced from each table felt like the contribution of the whole table, not any one person. And because table membership changed between each conversation in the Spirit, what surfaced from each table began to feel as if it was coming forth from the whole room.

Participants walked around the room to look for ideas that had surfaced multiple times in table conversations, as well as for points of difference. They also added to the newsprint anything important to them personally that had been lost in table note-taking. Mostly, the newsprint *had* captured what was most important from the conversations.

Participants were given three colored dots to place next to the phrases on the wall sheets they found most important or frequently mentioned in the discussions. During the final evening, the facilitators compiled and prioritized these phrases and words in a list and identified four potential proposals:

- Open the ministry of the Word to include more diverse voices in the preaching preparation process and the moment of preaching itself.

- Expand the role of lector to include eucharistic preaching. Or create a newly instituted ministry of lay preacher.
- Change Canon 767 to permit lay preaching at Eucharist with the local bishop's permission.
- Allow a period of experimentation suitable to the local context to explore expanded avenues for lay preaching.

On the final morning, the group received copies of this summary and a suggested template for crafting a group statement. Participants gathered themselves into four table groups to craft language in a template for each proposal. After ninety minutes, these templates were collected. During the last hour of the morning, the group identified two lead writers to write a single group statement based on the collected templates. The group also discussed how the joint statement would be edited and sent to the synod offices of the USCCB and the Vatican. The group also made plans to broadcast the common statement among friends and wider circles in the church.

After the March 2024 Symposium

Because the request for syntheses of synodal listening sessions by the USCCB had a deadline of April 8, 2024, the process of moving from a rough draft document to a solid statement that symposium participants could contribute to the synod process needed to happen quickly. The lead writers took the language the table groups suggested and continued refining it. The writers reworked the four proposals into two. Within a week, a draft statement was circulated via email to the first circle of readers for comment. The revised statement was circulated to the group within two weeks for additional response. Fr. Gregory Heille, OP, one of the symposium organizers, submitted the statement to the senior advisor for the synod at the USCCB and the synod secretariat in Rome. Within the next few weeks, the statement had been translated into Spanish, Italian, and French.

On the day the symposium closed, Pope Francis announced that some of the more controversial topics surfaced in "A Synodal Church in Mission" would be distributed for further reflection to ten study groups whose work would extend beyond the October 2024 general assembly. Heille also asked the synod secretariat to share the statement with the ministries study group that would address "some theological and canonical matters regarding specific ministerial forms."[8]

Dominicans often describe their vocation as *contemplare aliis tradere* (to hand to others the fruits of contemplation). For the colleagues participating in this symposium, the experience of conversation in the Spirit and the communal crafting of a statement "to hand on" was a profound expression of the Dominican charism at work at this most particular moment. The final version of the group's statement—shared in service of the synod's work—can be found below.

8. See Cindy Wooden, "Pope Sets up Groups to Study Most Controversial Issues Raised at Synod," Catholic News Service, March 14, 2024, https://www.usccb.org/news/2024/pope-sets-groups-study-most-controversial-issues-raised-synod.

Statement to the Synod on Synodality

A Proposal for Lay Eucharistic Preaching to Further a Synodal Church in Mission

> As each one has received a gift, use it to serve one another as good stewards of God's varied grace.
>
> —1 Peter 4:10 (ESV)

Part I. Our Work: Connecting Lay Preaching at the Eucharist to Synodality and Mission

The Dominican Preaching Network—a collaboration of three Dominican schools of preaching in the United States, Germany, and the Philippines—convened twenty-seven scholars and practitioners of preaching from March 11–14, 2024, to reflect on the guiding principle of "a synodal Church in mission" through the lens of lay eucharistic preaching. We conducted our work attending to synodal documents, specifically commissioned scholarly papers, listening and discussion sessions, panel presentations, and thematic analysis, all situated within a synodal listening process. We prayed together. We asked the Spirit's help. As a community, we now share the fruits of our discernment and submit them for further discernment by the Synod in October 2024 and the Synod's study group on "theological and canonical questions concerning specific forms of ministries."

Many lay ecclesial ministers discern a call from God and receive theological and ministerial training and formation to preach. Canon law permits lay preaching and yet restricts lay ecclesial ministers from receiving an ecclesial commission to preach the homily at Mass. We gathered as a group of theologians, ecclesiologists, preachers, and a canonist to consider this obstacle to lay preaching at Mass. Responding to the Synod's question about our Catholic identity as a synodal Church in mission, we now offer a constructive homiletic and ecclesiological appeal to charge or commission a more extensive and diverse pool of qualified lay preachers and evangelists to preach the Word of God at the Eucharist.

Part II. Convergences: Co-responsibility for the Ministry of the Word

We discovered among ourselves a remarkable number of places of deep agreement:

- The vocation of the baptized includes a share in the prophetic office of Christ; this office includes the proclamation of the Word.
- Within the Eucharistic celebration, an essential moment is the Liturgy of the Word: readings, Gospel proclamation, and homily. The Word arises within the gathered community, and the People of God hunger for both Eucharist and Word.

- That the gathered Assembly might attend ever more fully to God's Living Word made present in a liturgical communion between God and God's People in the Liturgy of the Word, the Church calls forth prepared liturgical ministers of the Word from within the Assembly—Lectors, Cantors, Catechists, and Preachers.

- The Eucharist, the source and summit of our life in Christ, is a synodal act. Therefore, the Church must listen to the voice of the Spirit and discern the many charisms for preaching in the community, given by the Spirit for the benefit of the Church to nourish those gathered at the Eucharistic table more fully.

- The task of the synodal Church is to listen humbly, speak boldly, and dialogue attentively, conscious that the Spirit gives multiple gifts/charisms for Eucharistic preaching. If the Church does not make efforts to discern charisms among the baptized, it cannot live fully its synodal identity.

- The Spirit is at work in preaching by diverse lay and ordained people from the centers and the margins, reflecting the variety of languages, genders, ethnicities, ages, races, social classes, sexualities, geographies, and cultures. We see the fruit already in diverse contexts, including churches and oratories; Eucharistic preaching is another appropriate context.

- The Church continues to experience an urgent and long-identified need for more effective proclamation of the Word and for preaching that reflects intercultural competence.

Part III. Our Proposals

To reflect a synodal Church more fully, we seek an opening of the ministry of the Word by incorporating a more comprehensive range of ministries under this umbrella. As scholars, theologians, and preachers, we believe that calling forth the *homiletic* preaching gifts of laypersons allows the Word of God to reach more people in a way that they can understand and connect to their experience. Specifically, our discernment leads us to two proposals:

1. Rather than waiting for a complete revision of canon law, **we propose to address the question of lay Eucharistic preaching canonically by an amendment to Canon 767 §1**, to read as follows:

    Can. 767 §1. Among the forms of preaching, the homily is distinguished by its placement within the Eucharistic celebration. In addition to concelebrating priests or deacons, properly prepared laity may be admitted to preach the homily, in accordance with the prescriptions of the Conference of Bishops.

2. In view of Item 1 above, **we propose expanding the use of installed ministries, such as Lector, Catechist, or a newly instituted ministry of Lay Preacher.** We believe that local communities need to call forth persons who might discern the preaching charism and receive formation to exercise this ministry in their Eucharistic Assemblies. Our ancient tradition records a lay ministry of Teacher or Reader that included proclaiming the Word and expounding on the Word in the liturgy (*The Apostolic Tradition* and the *Canons of Athanasius*). This tradition can be restored by enriching the currently instituted min-

istries of Lector and Catechist to include preaching and by instituting a new ministry of Lay Preacher. Pope Paul VI recovered the tradition of lay liturgical ministries by establishing the instituted ministries of Lector and Acolyte. Pope Francis further revitalized these ministries by opening them to women, instituting the ministry of Catechist, and calling for further development of lay ministries in local churches.

Liturgically, our proposals hold a promise to expand the theological understanding and ministerial reality of lay preaching at Eucharist; theologically, we invite a grounding away from the distinction between clergy and laity toward the relationships of community and ministry. Ecclesially, we seek a Church in which the baptismal call of every believer, given by the Spirit for the benefit of the Church, will be more fully realized, including the ministry of the layperson as preacher at Eucharist. Therefore, we submit our work to the Synod and its Ministries Study Group for further discernment, and we offer to assist in providing our theological study.

Submitted by Gregory Heille, OP, convener of the Symposium on the Pastoral Charge for Lay Catholic Eucharistic Preaching

Maxime Allard, OP, PhD, Dominican University College

Kayla August, MPS, Boston College

Kerstin-Marie Berretz, OP, DMin, *Institut für Pastoralhomiletik*

Mary Erika Bolaños, PhD, University of Santo Tomas

Wayne Cavalier, OP, PhD, Congar Institute for Ministry Development

Nathan Chase, PhD, Aquinas Institute of Theology

Elizabeth Donnelly, MTS, Catholic Women Preach

Megan Effron, MDiv, University of Notre Dame

Tom Esselman, CM, PhD, Vincentians Western Province

Sara Fairbanks, OP, PhD, Aquinas Institute of Theology

Ann Garrido, DMin, Aquinas Institute of Theology

Edward P. Hahnenberg, PhD, John Carroll University

Gregory Heille, OP, DMin, Aquinas Institute of Theology

Ruth Anne Henderson, OP, MA, European Lay Dominicans

Mary Catherine Hilkert, OP, PhD, University of Notre Dame

Layla Karst, PhD, Loyola Marymount University

Martin Madar, PhD, Xavier University

Megan McElroy, OP, DMin, Dominican Sisters of Grand Rapids

Maurice Nutt, CSsR, DMin, Aquinas Institute of Theology

F. Javier Orozco, PhD, Aquinas Institute of Theology

Barbara Reid, OP, PhD, Catholic Theological Union

Theresa Rickard, OP, DMin, Dominican Sisters of Blauvelt

Elissa Rinere, CP, JCD, Canonical Consultant

Casey Stanton, MDiv, Discerning Deacons

Mark Wedig, OP, PhD, Aquinas Institute of Theology

Deborah Wilhelm, DMin, Aquinas Institute of Theology

Carolyn Wright, DMin, Aquinas Institute of Theology

Theology of Ministry

A Theology of Ministry for Lay Eucharistic Preaching

Edward P. Hahnenberg

Can a theological case be made for the church to charge or commission a more extensive and diverse pool of qualified lay preachers and evangelists to preach the Word of God at the Eucharist? This question, around which the present volume revolves, is not asking whether laypeople can *preach the Gospel*. They can. The Second Vatican Council's "Dogmatic Constitution on the Church" and "Decree on the Apostolate of Lay People"—and every pope since—have made this clear.[1] The question is not whether laypeople can preach the Gospel *in a church or oratory*. Laypeople can do this, too. The 1983 Code of Canon Law explicitly says so (c. 766). Nor is the question whether laypeople can preach the Gospel in a church or oratory *in the context of a liturgical celebration*. They can. The *Directory for Sunday Celebrations in the Absence of a Priest*, the *Order of Celebrating*

1. Vatican II, *Lumen Gentium* 35; Vatican II, *Apostolicam Actuositatem* 6; Paul VI, *Evangelii Nuntiandi* 73; John Paul II, *Christifideles Laici* 33; Benedict XVI, *Verbum Domini* 94; Francis, *Evangelii Gaudium* 119–21.

Matrimony, and the *Order of Christian Funerals* allow lay preaching within these liturgical celebrations.[2]

The question at hand is whether laypeople can preach the Gospel in a church or oratory in the context of a celebration *of the Eucharist at the moment reserved for the homily*. Can laypeople do this? The answer to this more precise question is that laypeople *could* preach at the time of the homily—at least for a few years after the council—but now they cannot.[3] The current law on the question is clear. I will not rehearse it but will cite the US Conference of Catholic Bishops' 2001 "Complementary Norm to Canon 766," which states: "Preaching by the lay faithful may not take place within the Celebration of the Eucharist at the moment reserved for the homily." It further states that the diocesan bishop "may never dispense from the norm which reserves the homily to the sacred ministers."[4]

This canonical prohibition rests on an often implicit theology of ministry. In what follows, I examine this

2. Congregation for Divine Worship, *Directory for Sunday Celebrations in the Absence of a Priest* (Washington, DC: United States Catholic Conference, 1988); *Sunday Celebrations in the Absence of a Priest*, rev. ed. (Washington, DC: USCCB Publishing, 2012); *Order of Celebrating Matrimony* (Washington, DC: USCCB Publishing, 2016); *Order of Christian Funerals* (New York: Catholic Book Publishing, 1989).

3. Congregation for Divine Worship, *Directory for Masses with Children* (Washington, DC: United States Catholic Conference, 1974); Cardinal J. Wright to Cardinal J. Döpfner, November 20, 1973, in *Archiv für katholisches Kirchenrecht* 142 (1973): 480–82. See discussion in James H. Provost, "Brought Together by the Word of the Living God (Canons 762–772)," *Studia Canonica* 23 (1989): 345–71, at 354–59.

4. "USCCB Decree Implementing Canon 766 of the Code of Canon Law," USCCB Committee on the Liturgy Newsletter XXXVII (December 13, 2001): 49–50.

underlying theology and offer an alternative approach, one more consonant with the ecclesiological vision of Vatican II, to articulate a theology that supports the ministry of lay eucharistic preaching.

In developing such a theology, it is important to distinguish theological arguments for and against *lay eucharistic preaching* from theological arguments for and against *expanding access to ordination*. To clarify what I mean, consider the following thought experiment. Imagine that current disciplinary and doctrinal restrictions on who can be admitted to the sacrament of holy orders were suddenly lifted and that all ordained ministries—deacon, presbyter, and bishop—along with their corresponding offices, were now open, in principle, to all baptized members of the people of God, including women and married men. Imagine that the giant tourniquet constraining our conversation was removed, and the sacramental grace of ordination was allowed to flow freely to every member of the Body of Christ. Would we still want to make an argument for lay eucharistic preaching? Yes. I would still make this case because I argue that lay eucharistic preaching is an appropriate and authentic ministry, regardless of who is and is not included among the ordained.

I draw here on Edward Schillebeeckx, who years ago made a distinction between an *authentic* multiplicity of ministries (those that arise out of new needs in the community) and an *inauthentic* multiplicity of ministries (those that occur because access to the appropriate ministries is withheld from individuals and groups in the church).[5] If lay eucharistic preaching is an *inauthentic* diversification of ministry—because, the argument goes,

5. Edward Schillebeeckx, *Ministry: Leadership in the Community of Jesus Christ*, trans. John Bowden (New York: Crossroad, 1981), 78.

eucharistic preaching belongs properly or intrinsically to the ordained alone—then it would be better either to prohibit it or to avoid it by *ordaining* these men and women so that they can preach in this way! However, if lay eucharistic preaching is an *authentic* diversification of ministry, which I understand it to be, then theological arguments for it have an enduring value. The case for lay eucharistic preaching would still stand even if the ranks of the ordained included women and men, married, single, and professed.

The argument that follows takes the form of a medieval disputation. Since Aquinas Institute of Theology sponsored the symposium for this volume, I thought it appropriate to adopt the style of the Angelic Doctor. Like Thomas Aquinas's approach in the *Summa Theologica*, I will begin with objections, offer my response, and then reply to the objections. In the spirit of the *Summa*, my intent is not to close off the conversation but to open it up.

Objections to Lay Eucharistic Preaching

Can appropriately prepared and qualified lay members of the Christian faithful be allowed to preach the Word of God at Eucharist?

Objection 1. It seems not. According to the Second Vatican Council, the homily is "part of the liturgy itself."[6]

6. *Sacrosanctum Concilium* ("Constitution on the Sacred Liturgy" [SC]) 52. English translations of Vatican II documents are taken from Austin Flannery, ed., *Vatican Council II: The Basic Sixteen Documents; Constitutions, Decrees, Declarations*, A Completely Revised Translation in Inclusive Language (Collegeville, MN: Liturgical Press, 2014).

Given its eucharistic context, the homily differs from all other forms of preaching the Word of God. All preaching falls within the prophetic function of the church as a way in which the Christian community participates in Christ's threefold work as priest, prophet, and king. However, the homily, by its place in the eucharistic liturgy, is also an exercise of the priestly function of Christ. According to canon lawyer John Chrysostom Kozlowski, OP, "Thus, while not wishing or attempting to strictly divide the three-fold *munera* of Christ—priest, prophet, and king—the liturgy, including the homily, is primarily an act of Christ the priest."[7] Although the homily is not an essential part of the liturgy (a Eucharist without a homily is still a Eucharist), the homily is essentially liturgical. It is primarily an act of worship. As an integral part of the eucharistic sacrifice, the homily belongs to the one who offers this sacrifice on behalf of the community: the ordained priest.

The liturgical nature of the homily—and thus the unique responsibility of the ordained priest for the homily—is confirmed by Vatican II's repeated emphasis on the unity of the Liturgy of the Word and the Liturgy of the Eucharist—the two tables of the one liturgical celebration (SC 48, 51). *Sacrosanctum Concilium* teaches that the two parts that make up the Mass "are so closely connected with each other that they form but one single act of worship" (SC 56). Therefore, the one who presides

7. John Chrysostom Kozlowski, "The Laity and Liturgical Preaching: What Are the Necessary Theological and Canonical Requirements?," *The Jurist* 72 (2012): 240–69, at 261. Kozlowski relies on Joseph Fox, "The Homily and the Authentic Interpretation of Canon 767.1," *Apollinaris* 62 (1989): 123–69, at 135–42. See SC 7.

over the Liturgy of the Eucharist presides over the Liturgy of the Word, including preaching the homily. Lay members of the Christian faithful cannot preside over the Liturgy of the Eucharist; thus, it seems they cannot be allowed to preach the Word of God at the Eucharist.

Objection 2. Furthermore, the prohibition of lay eucharistic preaching follows not only from the nature of the liturgy but also from the nature of the ordained ministry. Ordination configures the priest to Christ the head. It thus gives the ordained priest a participation in Christ's prophetic, priestly, and royal work that differs essentially from the configuration to Christ brought about by baptism. Reserving eucharistic preaching to the ordained affirms the unity of word, sacrament, and community leadership that follows from the priest's unique participation in the work of Christ.[8] The 1997 interdicasterial instruction *Ecclesiae de Mysterio* states that the exclusion of the nonordained faithful from preaching the homily "is not based on the preaching ability of sacred ministers nor their theological preparation, but on that function which is reserved to them in virtue of having received the sacrament of Holy Orders." It explains that bishops cannot dispense from the norm because "it is not merely a disciplinary law but one which touches upon the closely connected functions of teaching and sanctifying."[9] The document expands on this last point

8. See discussion in Mary Catherine Hilkert, *Naming Grace: Preaching and the Sacramental Imagination* (New York: Continuum, 1997), 158–65.

9. Congregation for the Clergy et al., "Instruction on Certain Questions Regarding the Collaboration of the Non-Ordained Faithful in the Sacred Ministry of Priest" (*Ecclesiae de Mysterio*) (August 15, 1997), art. 3.1.

in its section on theological principles, which asserts, "The functions of the ordained minister, taken as a whole, constitute a single indivisible unity in virtue of their singular foundation in Christ."[10] The unity of the eucharistic liturgy is distinct from but intimately related to the unity of the pastoral ministry of the priest, who presides over not two distinct activities, Word and sacrament, but "one integral act offered by the one person, Jesus Christ, as priest."[11] Thus, it seems that lay members of the Christian faithful may not preach the Word of God at the Eucharist.

Lay Eucharistic Preaching in an Ordered Communion

On the other hand, Vatican II's "Decree on the Apostolate of Lay People" (*Apostolicam Actuositatem*) says that "the true apostle is on the lookout for occasions to proclaim Christ by word, either to unbelievers to draw them towards the faith, or to the faithful to instruct them, strengthen them, call them to a more fervent life" (6).

The Authority to Preach

Reply: A study of the history of lay preaching surfaces different answers to the question of what grounds the authority to preach. While I like to believe that all parties presume that the ultimate ground of preaching is the commission of Christ to proclaim the Gospel, how that commission is mediated to the individual preacher is highly contested. One strand in the tradition argues

10. Congregation for the Clergy et al., "Instruction on Certain Questions" 2.

11. Fox, "Homily," 149.

that the authority to preach comes from the preacher receiving proper jurisdiction from the church's hierarchy. Another strand contends that the authority to preach comes from ordination, with jurisdiction to preach either implied or a *pro forma* companion to holy orders. A third strand argues that the authority to preach comes from the *vita apostolica*—a charism grounded in the preacher's radical commitment to living the gospel life in imitation of the earliest apostles.[12] The acquiescence of medieval monks to the claims of the canons regular may have shifted the emphasis to ordination as the source of preaching authority. In contrast, the thirteenth-century debates between the regular clergy and the mendicants may have shifted the emphasis to jurisdiction and canonical mission.[13] The critical point is that, in this history, legislation surrounding lay preaching was almost always a response to particular historical circumstances (such as widespread theological illiteracy) and concrete challenges (such as heretical movements or clergy disputes). More often than not, the theological rationale followed as an attempt to understand or justify political and pastoral agendas.

12. Patrick F. Norris, "Lay Preaching and Canon Law: Who May Give a Homily?," *Studia Canonica* 24 (1990): 443–54, at 447. See Mary Catherine Hilkert, "Women Preaching the Gospel," *Theology Digest* 33 (1986): 423–40; Edward Schillebeeckx, "The Right of Every Christian to Speak in Light of Evangelical Experience 'In the Midst of Brothers and Sisters,'" in *Preaching and the Non-Ordained: An Interdisciplinary Study*, ed. Nadine Foley (Collegeville, MN: Liturgical Press, 1983), 11–29; Elissa Rinere, "Authorization for Lay Preaching in the Church" (JCL thesis, Washington, DC, The Catholic University of America, 1981).

13. See Schillebeeckx, "Right of Every Christian," 16–32.

What grounds the authority to preach? Vatican II did not consider this question a major focus of its deliberations. However, it did articulate several theological principles that would have implications for this question—including the specific question of the authority of the nonordained to preach.

The Second Vatican Council repeatedly affirmed that all Christian faithful participate in the prophetic work of Christ, and they do so based on their baptism, membership in the Body of Christ, and the gifts of the Holy Spirit.[14] Laypeople exercise this prophetic mission in the very living of their lives of faith. However, as *Apostolicam Actuositatem* states, this witness of life "is not the sole element in the apostolate; the true apostle is on the lookout for occasions to proclaim Christ by word" (AA 6). Laypeople, as much as the ordained, echo the apostle Paul, "'Woe to me if I do not preach the Gospel' (1 Cor 9:16)" (AA 6). In terms of the source of this apostolate, the council is clear: "Lay people's right and duty to be apostles derives from their union with Christ their head. Inserted as they are in the mystical body of Christ by baptism and strengthened by the power of the holy Spirit in confirmation, it is by the Lord himself that they are assigned to the apostolate" (AA 3). Moreover, within this broad ministry of the Word, the council opens the door to lay liturgical preaching—if only in an initial, hesitant way. *Apostolicam Actuositatem* states, "Finally, the hierarchy entrusts the laity with certain tasks more closely connected with the duties of pastors: in the teaching of

14. See *Lumen Gentium* 12, 17, 31, 33, 35; *Dei Verbum* 10; *Gaudium et Spes* 41; *Apostolicam Actuositatem* 2, 3, 6, 10, 25.

christian doctrine, for example, in certain liturgical actions, in the care of souls" (AA 24).[15]

Vatican II's Ecclesiological Imagination and a Preconciliar Priesthood

The council's teaching on the laity falls within a more extensive reshaping of the ecclesiological imagination at Vatican II. While the council did not endorse a single, comprehensive ecclesiological model, it consistently affirmed themes that moved beyond the triumphalism, clericalism, and juridicalism that marred preconciliar theologies of church.[16] These themes included the biblical view of the church as the people of God and the Body of Christ, the affirmation of the priesthood of all the faithful, the notion of charisms as ordinary and pervasive, the idea of baptism as initiation into a community and its mission, and the participation of all believers in the priestly, prophetic, and royal work of Christ.

These conciliar themes, recovered from the tradition, inspired a shift in the Catholic imagination of church and were no longer equated with clergy. No longer was the mission of Christ imagined as bestowed from above on the apostles, trickling down to bishops and priests, and sometimes shared with the laity. The council's emphasis on baptism and active participation helps to explain the explosion of lay ministries following

15. See also *Lumen Gentium* 33, 35, 41; *Apostolicam Actuositatem* 22; *Ad Gentes* 15–17, 23, 24, 26.

16. See the intervention by Bishop Emil Josef De Smedt cited in Giuseppe Ruggieri, "The Schema on the Church," in *History of Vatican II*, ed. Giuseppe Alberigo and Joseph A. Komonchak (Maryknoll, NY: Orbis Books, 2006), 2:337.

the council, including the expansion of lay preaching. The council's confidence that all Christians share in the prophetic office of Christ helps to explain the openings to lay liturgical preaching—and even lay eucharistic preaching—that marked the postconciliar period. These conciliar themes even help to explain the liberal legislation of the 1983 Code on lay participation in the ministry of the Word (c. 759) and on lay preaching in a church or oratory (c. 766).

But does the ecclesiological vision of the Second Vatican Council explain the reservation of eucharistic preaching to the ordained? Canon 766 is followed immediately by canon 767, where the dynamism toward greater inclusion of the laity in preaching hits a roadblock at the homily. Why? Was canon 767 simply a line in the sand or a line of sandbags stacked up to protect the privileges of the ordained that Rome worried were being washed away in the postconciliar period? Without impugning motives or suspecting bad faith, it does appear here that a dissonant note is sounded that grates against the overall ecclesiological vision of the council. The two objections noted at the start are significant. Insofar as there are theological arguments behind the canonical reservation, they are rooted in the retention of a medieval or Tridentine theology of priesthood that consolidates ministry under the aura of the ordained priest, understood within a cultic-sacerdotal framework.

We can see the theological tension between this theology of priesthood and the council's ecclesiology in the evolution of the law after Vatican II. Even as the Congregation for Clergy gave permission to the German bishops for laypeople to preach at Mass, Cardinal Wright wrote to Cardinal Döpfner that the congregation shared the same concern expressed by the German bishops: "That problem is: whether extending the office of preaching to the laity will obscure the essential distinction existing between the ministerial priesthood of priests and the universal priesthood of believers. . . . This applies especially to lay preaching during the Mass: the liturgy of the word and the liturgy of the eucharist are so closely connected that they form but a single act of worship and in the Mass of the community the priest exercises not only his ministry of word and sacrifice but also his office as pastor of the people."[17]

In the preparation of the 1983 Code, the question of lay eucharistic preaching was explicitly addressed. In these discussions, a sharp distinction was made between preaching in general and preaching the homily at Mass. This distinction allowed the drafters of the Code to affirm lay preaching, but prohibit lay eucharistic preaching. The reason for this distinction reflects a strong association between Word, sacrifice, and the *sacerdos* who offers both. Records from the study group revising these canons reveal a consensus that lay preaching within the Mass is prohibited "because there is some equation between the Mass, which pertains to the priest, and the preaching of the divine Word." Later, the reporter notes that lay preaching of the homily is expressly excluded "since the homily is a magisterial act which also has a cultic aspect, since it is a part of the liturgy."[18]

17. Cited in Fox, "Homily," 148n49.

18. *Coetus Studiorum "De magisterio ecclesiastico,"* Session 8 (October 13–17, 1975), Can. 18 (CIC 1342), cited in Fox, "Homily," 157–58n61.

The 1997 Vatican instruction, tellingly titled "Instruction on Certain Questions Regarding the Collaboration of the Non-Ordained Faithful in the Sacred Ministry of Priest," represents an extreme example of a theology of the sacred minister in which the entire ministerial life of the church is subsumed into the ministry of the ordained: "A person is not a minister simply in performing a task, but through sacramental ordination. Only the Sacrament of Orders gives the ordained minister a particular participation in the office of Christ, the Shepherd and Head in his Eternal Priesthood."[19] The closely connected functions of teaching and sanctifying—of Word and sacrifice—prohibit the laity from ever preaching the homily.

Ordered Ministries within an Ordered Communion

To advance lay eucharistic preaching requires overcoming this sacralized theology of priesthood by situating the ordained ministry within a broader theology of ministry in line with the council's ecclesiological vision. Fortunately, a lot of good work has been done over the past sixty years on a theology of ministry that is faithful to the council. I point to one strand in a rich conversation by highlighting a theology of ordered ministries within the church understood as an ordered communion.

Shortly after the Second Vatican Council, the Dominican theologian, ecumenist, and council *peritus* Yves Congar looked back on his earlier writings on the laity and acknowledged the limitations of his preconciliar work. In light of the council's ecclesiological revolution,

19. Congregation for the Clergy et al., "Instruction on Certain Questions" 2, citing John Paul II, *Christifideles Laici* 23.

Congar saw that he had inadvertently started with a hierarchical premise by beginning with the laity. Thus, he could not help but treat the laity over and against the clergy. What if instead of starting with the split between two groups within the church, Congar continued, one was to begin with the unity of the whole baptismal community? He then asked how a diversity of ministries serves this community and its mission in the world. Congar concluded that the decisive pair for a theology of ministry was not "clergy-laity" but "ministries-community."[20] In that line, Congar captured a fundamental paradigm shift following the council—from a dividing-line model of church and ministries to a model of concentric circles.[21]

Congar had little patience for exclusively Christocentric ecclesiologies that imagined Christ establishing the hierarchy by appointing the Twelve, who established the community. But he also critiqued overly charismatic ecclesiologies wherein the free movement of the Spirit spawned whatever church offices served a good purpose.[22] Congar sought to balance the traditional affirmation that Christ instituted the church with the insight that the Holy Spirit is a co-instituting principle. Congar recognized the need to balance institution with charism, order with communion. He spoke of Christ willing a

20. Yves Congar, "My Path-Findings in the Theology of Laity and Ministries," *The Jurist* 32 (1972): 169–88, at 176.

21. See Thomas F. O'Meara, *Theology of Ministry*, rev. ed. (New York: Paulist Press, 1999), and Edward P. Hahnenberg, *Ministries: A Relational Approach* (New York: Crossroad, 2003).

22. See Yves Congar, *I Believe in the Holy Spirit*, trans. David Smith (New York: Seabury Press, 1983), 2:9.

"structured community" within which various ministries functioned.[23]

If the church is a structured community or an ordered communion, then within it are *ordered ministries*. The diverse ministries within the community are not an undifferentiated mass. There are distinctions, and these distinctions are important—but they cannot be reduced to the ontological change that occurs at ordination. Another way of saying this is that the problem with the clergy-laity distinction is that it is too blunt of a divide to capture the diversity of ministries serving Church and world. Several contemporary Catholic theologians have turned to the category of "ordered ministry" to capture this diversity. Ordered ministry is broader than ordained ministry but narrower than Christian discipleship. Ordered ministry includes the ordained ministries. It also includes lay ecclesial ministers serving full time as catechetical leaders, youth ministers, pastoral associates, and many other roles. Ordered ministry also includes occasional ministries, such as eucharistic ministers, retreat leaders, outreach coordinators, and other volunteers. It does not include every act of service performed out of Christian charity. Those are good and important and appropriately called ministries. What makes a ministry an ordered ministry is a combination of vocational call, public role, and communal recognition—all of which together move the individual disciple into a new set of relationships within the public ministerial life of the church.

Richard Gaillardetz, Susan Wood, and I have all argued that the reality of ordered ministry in the church in the United States today includes three basic categories—

23. Congar, "My Path-Findings," 177.

ordained ministries, full-time lay ecclesial ministries, and volunteer ministries—each of which corresponds to a different ritual entrance into ministry.[24] These liturgical commissionings are already a part of our Catholic tradition: (1) blessing as commissioning, (2) installation or institution, and (3) ordination. If baptism is the liturgical rite that initiates one into the ministerial community, it does not position the Christian disciple into an ordered ministry. Further liturgical designation is needed to *name*—a recognition that is also a strengthening—those public ministries exercised on behalf of the community. They are best called by their liturgical entrance—commissioned ministers, instituted ministers, and ordained ministers—all representing different degrees of ordered ministry within the church.

These diverse ministries are best understood in thoroughly relational terms. What makes someone an *ordered* minister is not *who* does it, *what* they do, or *how* they are authorized, but a combination of all three. The coming together of vocational commitment, public ministry, and official recognition brings the minister into a new position within the community. Gaillardetz called this "ecclesial repositioning" and included within it not only the ordained ministries of bishop, presbyter, and deacon but also other lay ministries: "Here I have in mind not just the ordained ministries but, for example, the director of Christian formation mentioned earlier. This 'lay' min-

24. See Richard R. Gaillardetz, "Shifting Meanings in the Lay-Clergy Distinction," *Irish Theological Quarterly* 64 (1999): 115–39; Hahnenberg, *Ministries*; Susan K. Wood, ed., *Ordering the Baptismal Priesthood: Theologies of Lay and Ordained Ministry* (Collegeville, MN: Liturgical Press, 2003).

ister is called by the community, based on a recognized charism, to take a new public role in the Church. She is called to enter into a new ministerial relationship within the community. This new ministerial relationship may or may not be ritualized, but the repositioning is clear and obvious to those active in her community."[25]

In my view, such a relational approach to ministry avoids the pitfalls of both heavily ontological and heavily functional theologies of ministry. It transcends overly Christocentric and overly Spirit-centric accounts with a thoroughly relational, trinitarian theology of ministry.[26]

A Theology of Ministry for Lay Eucharistic Preaching

What does all of this mean for lay eucharistic preaching?

First, a relational approach to ministry steers us away from considering *who* preaches at Eucharist either in terms of ontology alone (i.e., the one who is ordained preaches) or in terms of function alone (i.e., the one who has the charism for preaching preaches). Instead, the one who preaches at Eucharist is the one who exists within a particular set of ecclesial relationships—who holds a specific ecclesial position—within the eucharistic community. This position is a function of who they are, what they do, *and* how the community and its leaders recognize them. All of these, taken together, shape the ecclesial position of the minister. The primary factor in discerning the appropriate minister to preach at the community's Eucharist is neither ordination nor ability but the minister's relationship with the community.

25. Gaillardetz, "Shifting Meanings," 135.

26. Hahnenberg, *Ministries,* 76–98.

Second, a relational approach to ministry opens up a fresh consideration of the power of jurisdiction. Vatican II's desire to overcome the separation of the power of orders and the power of jurisdiction had a positive impact on the theology of the episcopate in that it theologically grounded the total ministry of the bishop as prophet, priest, and king in episcopal ordination, not papal delegation. However, the council's reuniting of orders and jurisdiction had a negative impact on the lay apostolate. It created a certain ambiguity around the canonical question of how laity cooperate in the power of governance (c. 129 §2). This is not unrelated to the question of lay preaching. Recall the historical debates over the source of the authority to preach. Does the authority come from the sacrament (orders) or from a canonical mission (jurisdiction)? By framing a theology of ministry in relational terms, we move away from conceiving authorization in terms of a "power" that is held by the individual (e.g., he "received" the faculty to preach), and we move toward an understanding of jurisdiction as a form of communion with the ecclesial community. Thus, the canonical is communal, following a theology of communion. Whether talking about ordained or lay preachers, there is a general consensus that (1) the ministry of preaching has a sacramental source and (2) it is exercised in union with the church understood as a structured community. The first claim is theological. The second is canonical. Both are important. The church cannot endorse rogue bishops with no accountability to the universal Church. Neither can the church endorse lay ecclesial ministers who imagine themselves as independent contractors serving their own clientele. Jurisdiction, governance, and authorization are all relational categories.

Third, a theology of ordered ministries aligns well with Pope Francis's attempt to revive instituted lay ministries in local churches worldwide. As is well known, Pope Paul VI officially instituted lay ministries of lector and acolyte in 1973 as part of the postconciliar reform of the minor orders. This bold ministerial reconfiguration failed to have a real pastoral impact, mainly because Paul VI reserved these new lay ministries to men. That restriction meant that almost no one outside of a seminary was ever officially instituted in a lay ministry—even as laywomen and laymen widely took up the *functions* of lector and acolyte.[27]

Pope Francis removed Paul VI's restriction with his *motu proprio*, *Spiritus Domini* in January 2021, opening up the officially instituted ministries of lector and acolyte to women. Four months later, with *Antiquum Ministerium*, he established the lay ministry of catechist for the universal Church—asking all episcopal conferences to make this ministry effective in their local contexts.[28] These moves offer great promise for fostering official ministerial structures to support a variety of lay ministries, including the ministry of lay preaching. However, one problem with these instituted lay ministries, at least for American Catholics, is that Americans typically use the words lector, acolyte, and catechist primarily in reference to volunteers—who usually receive minimal preparation and serve only occasionally. In *Antiquum Ministerium* and the accompanying instructions, Pope

27. On this history, see Hahnenberg, *Ministries*, 183–93.

28. Pope Francis, *Antiquum Ministerium* ("Instituting the Ministry of Catechist"), Apostolic Letter Issued "Motu Proprio" (May 10, 2021) 9.

Francis lays out a more robust vision of a vocationally committed, usually full-time, well-prepared minister who exercises stable ministerial leadership in the local church, serving in close mutual collaboration with the ordained. This vision reflects the reality of lay ecclesial ministry in the United States. By formally instituting the ministry of catechist, Pope Francis offers an official (canonical) recognition of the ecclesial position these ministers already enjoy within their communities.

Is this not the perfect opportunity for imagining an officially instituted ministry of lay preacher, who, like the presbyter and deacon, would receive the faculty to preach at the liturgical entrance into their ministry? In his August 15, 2022, message commemorating the fiftieth anniversary of *Ministeria Quaedam*, the apostolic letter by which Paul VI created the first instituted ministries, Pope Francis called the whole Church to an open and creative reconsideration of lay ministries. He reminded bishops of their duty to order ministries—pointing out that, fifty years earlier, Paul VI had invited episcopal conferences to propose other instituted lay ministries that they considered necessary or useful in their territories. In a message on the fiftieth anniversary of *Ministeria Quaedam*, Francis described the structuring or ordering of ministries as "not merely functional but rather a careful communitarian discernment, born of listening to what the Spirit suggests to the Church in one concrete place and in the present moment of her life." Every ministerial structure "born of this discernment is dynamic, living and flexible, like the working of the Spirit."[29] Pope

29. Pope Francis, "Message on the Fiftieth Anniversary of the Apostolic Letter Issued 'Motu Proprio' *Ministeria Quaedam* of Saint Paul VI" (August 15, 2022) 4.

Francis acknowledged that further theological reflection was needed on everything from the proper terminology to the doctrinal and juridical implications. However, he warned that we should not wait until every issue is defined and resolved before "experiencing the lived reality of these ministries." If we did, we would never get anywhere. Citing *Evangelii Gaudium*, the pope repeated, "Realities are more important than ideas."[30]

Francis concluded this remarkable letter by expressing his hope to start a dialogue with the episcopal conferences on this topic "to share the richness of the Church's ministerial experiences in these past fifty years."[31] This conversation, the pope affirmed, is particularly important in the context of the current synodal journey. Just over a year later, the synthesis report of the first session of the Synod on Synodality offered the following concrete proposal: "We need more creativity in establishing ministries according to the needs of local churches, with the particular involvement of the young. One can think of further expanding responsibilities assigned to the existing ministry of lector, responsibilities that are already broader than those performed in the liturgy. This could become a fuller ministry of the Word of God, which, in appropriate contexts, could also include preaching."[32] Perhaps one of these "appropriate contexts" for the lay ministry of preaching is within the eucharistic celebration at the moment reserved for the homily.

30. Francis, *Ministeria Quaedam* 8.

31. Francis, *Ministeria Quaedam* 10.

32. XVI Ordinary General Assembly of the Synod of Bishops, Synthesis Report for the First Session, "A Synodal Church in Mission" (Vatican City: October 4–29, 2023), Part II, 8.n.

Conclusion: Reply to Objections

I promised a disputation, so I owe my readers replies to the two objections I raised at the start. So, in good Thomistic fashion, I offer the same anticlimactic end found in every article of the *Summa*.

Reply to Objection 1. In response to the argument that the unity of the liturgy implies that it is most fitting that the one who presides over the table of the Eucharist also presides over the table of the Word, including the homily, we can note that while priestly ordination is absolutely intrinsic to the consecration of the eucharistic elements, it is not absolutely intrinsic to eucharistic preaching. This is evidenced by the allowances for past lay eucharistic preaching and diaconal eucharistic preaching in the present. Moreover, an ideal is not a binding norm. So, while the ideal may be that the presider preaches the homily at Mass, this ideal can admit exceptions, such as when a concelebrating priest or even a priest who is not concelebrating is invited to preach.

Reply to Objection 2. The "single indivisible unity" of the ordained minister's priestly, prophetic, and royal functions follows from his unique participation in the role of Christ as head of the church.[33] However, the ability to act in the person of Christ the head belongs to the ordained priest—presbyter and bishop—but not to the deacon. As *Lumen Gentium* states, deacons "receive the imposition of hands 'not for the priesthood, but for the ministry'" (LG 29). Pope Benedict XVI was careful to protect this distinction in his 2009 revisions to the Code of Canon Law,

33. Congregation for the Clergy et al., "Instruction on Certain Questions" 2.

which included amendments to canons 1008 and 1009 that removed language associating the deacon with acting in the person of Christ the head.[34] Thus, the appeal to the "single indivisible unity" of the priestly ministry based on his acting in the person of Christ the head does not support allowing the deacon to preach the homily. But if the deacon can preach the homily, as canonical legislation allows, this argument would not prevent other non-priestly ministers—instituted or extraordinary—from preaching the homily. Moreover, even in the case of the ordained priest, the unity of the ordained minister's priestly, prophetic, and royal functions does not mean that one minister always needs to do everything. Such is not the case for reading the Scriptures, singing the psalm, or offering the prayers of the faithful at Mass. To preside over the eucharistic liturgy does not mean to monopolize. The task of a good presider is to call forth gifts from others in the assembly, including those with the gift to preach.

34. Benedict XVI, *Omnium in Mentem* (October 26, 2009), in *AAS* 102 (2010): 8–10, cited in Kozlowski, "Laity and Liturgical Preaching," 262n76.

Lay Preaching as an Authentic Multiplication of Ministries

Nathan P. Chase

Edward Hahnenberg has provided an excellent exposition of the theology of ministry, particularly the arguments for and against lay preaching. In the process, I think he rightly argued that the issue is fundamentally about ministry. I want to take up a question that Hahnenberg introduced toward the beginning of his paper: "Imagine that current disciplinary and doctrinal restrictions on who can be admitted to the sacrament of holy orders were suddenly lifted and that all ordained ministries . . . were now open, in principle, to all baptized members of the people of God. . . . Would we still want to make an argument for lay eucharistic preaching?" He then goes on to borrow the distinction by Edward Schillebeeckx about an authentic and inauthentic multiplicity of ministries, the former arising "out of new needs in the community" and the latter from the withholding of a ministry from individuals in the church.[1] To answer his question in light of this distinction, I think the clear

1. Edward Schillebeeckx, *Ministry: Leadership in the Community of Jesus Christ*, trans. John Bowden (New York: Crossroad, 1981), 78.

answer is Yes! Yes, we would still want to argue for lay eucharistic preaching.

I would argue that even with a broadening of ordained ministry, we should still consider lay preaching at the Eucharist precisely because this is an authentic ministry in the church that is very much needed today. For this reason, I want to focus my response on the authentic multiplication of ministries in the early church and how the documents after Vatican II, namely, *Ministeria Quaedam,* sought to crack open the door to a diversity of ministry. This focus will provide some historical context to push forward Pope Francis's recent moves in *Spiritus Domini*[2] and *Antiquum Ministerium,*[3] which have sought to reevaluate ministry in the church in light of a diversity of gifts and functions.

Historical Diversity of Ministries

Here, it is worth surveying some historical evidence for the existence of an authentic multiplicity of ministries in the early church. One needs to look only at the early descriptions of ministries in the documents known as the "church orders,"[4] written between the second and fourth centuries, to see the diversity of ministry but also

2. Pope Francis, *Spiritus Domini* ("Modifying Canon 230 §1 of the Code of Canon Law Regarding Access of Women to the Ministries of Lector and Acolyte"), Apostolic Letter Issued "Motu Propio" (January 10, 2021).

3. Pope Francis, "Message on the Fiftieth Anniversary of the Apostolic Letter Issued 'Motu Proprio' *Ministeria Quaedam* of Saint Paul VI" (August 15, 2022).

4. Paul Bradshaw, *Ancient Church Orders,* Joint Liturgical Studies 80 (Norwich, UK: Hymns Ancient and Modern, 2015).

the seeds of later conflicts between what we would call the "ordained" and "instituted" ministers.

The Apostolic Tradition can serve as a perfect example. This church order is dated in its final form by most scholars to the fourth century, but it likely preserves some practices as early as the second century. Concerning its provenance, it appears to be a collection of liturgical materials from different geographical locations.[5] The document outlines two types of ministries: (1) the ordained—bishops, presbyters, and deacons—and (2) the nonordained—confessors, subdeacons, readers, widows, healers, virgins, teachers, and stewards. In some cases, such as among the confessors, widows, healers, and teachers, there were attempts by the ordained ministries (those in authority) to subjugate these more charismatic ministries to the more institutionalized ministries of the bishop, presbyter, and deacon.[6] I will not go into this tension between institutionalized and more charismatic ministries. However, the history of ministry in the church—particularly the ministry of preaching—has, I believe, constantly been beset by tensions between those who feel called to a ministry by God and the desire of those in authority to institutionalize that call. We might borrow from Avery Dulles's distinction between the

5. For the text and a commentary on the text, see Paul Bradshaw, Maxwell E. Johnson, and L. Edward Phillips, *The Apostolic Tradition: A Commentary*, Hermeneia (Minneapolis: Fortress Press, 2002). For an alternative dating and provenance, see Alistair Stewart, *On the Apostolic Tradition*, 2nd ed. (Crestwood, NY: St. Vladimir's Seminary Press, 2015).

6. Bradshaw, Johnson, and Phillips, *Apostolic Tradition*, 67, 71, 80, 84, 102, 189–90, and 206–7.

prophetic and institutional church in his work *Models of the Church*.[7]

For our purposes, I want to focus on two ministries in *The Apostolic Tradition*: the reader and the teacher. The reader is explicitly named only in chapter 11 of the document. The chapter describes the establishment of the office but not its function, though its function is apparent. Interestingly, the office of reader was unknown in the ancient West, except in some Gallican sources, which are dependent on the *Statuta Ecclesiae Antiqua*, which is itself dependent on *The Apostolic Tradition*.[8] The Egyptian church, which was heavily influenced by *The Apostolic Tradition*, provides additional information about this office. According to the Egyptian *Canons of Athanasius*, which date from the late fourth or early fifth century, the reader could also fulfill a teaching function in the church.[9] In modern terms, this teaching function would have been some mixture of a catechist and a preacher. Teachers receive a similar ministerial function

7. Avery Dulles, *Models of the Church*, exp. ed. (New York: Doubleday, 2002).

8. Bradshaw, Johnson, and Phillips, *Apostolic Tradition*, 75.

9. See canon 58 in the Arabic and Coptic in Wilhelm Riedel and W. E. Crum, *The Canons of Athanasius of Alexandria: The Arabic and Coptic Versions* (London: Williams and Norgate, 1904), 37 (Arabic) and 126 (Coptic). Ewa Wipszycka, "Les ordres mineurs dans l'Église d'Égypte du IVe au VIIIe siècle," *The Journal of Juristic Papyrology* 23 (1993): 197. For more on the dating and provenance of this text, see Ewa Wipszycka, "A Certain Bishop and a Certain Diocese in Egypt at the Turn of the Fourth and Fifth Centuries: The Testimony of the Canons of Athanasius," *U Schyłku Starożytności: Studia Źródłoznawcze—Late Antiquity: Studies in Source Criticism* 17/18 (2019): 91–115.

in *The Apostolic Tradition*.[10] Chapters 18 and 19 describe a prayer service where the teachers instruct the faithful and the catechumens.[11] While the exact liturgical context in which these ministers appeared to have preached is unclear, a eucharistic context cannot be ruled out. In early documents like *The Apostolic Tradition*, we see a diversity of ministries based on the community's needs, and at least two of these—reader and teacher—performed a type of preaching function.

The medieval period saw a reification of ministry, particularly in the Latin West, leading to a clear distinction between the "major" and "minor" orders. The former were the ordained offices of bishop, presbyter, and deacon (and subdeacon), and the latter were the orders of porter, exorcist, lector, and acolyte. These minor orders were seen as "grades of the one priesthood centered around the eucharist; they were stepping stones on the way to presbyteral ordination."[12] Only the major orders (bishop, priest, and deacon) and the minor orders were allowed to exercise any functions during the liturgy. Increasingly, these minor orders, which had once been the purview of all the baptized as seen in *The Apostolic Tradition*, were confined to only those destined for presbyteral ordination, which had the effect of clericalizing these orders.

At the same time, this did not prevent other authentic offices needed by the community to emerge. The ministry of the catechist is a perfect example. Catechists became especially important in the post-Tridentine period

10. This ministry appears in chaps. 15, 18, 19, and 41.1–3.

11. Bradshaw, Johnson, and Phillips, *Apostolic Tradition*, 100–103.

12. Edward Hahnenberg, *Ministries: A Relational Approach* (New York: Crossroad, 2003), 157.

alongside the larger turn to catechesis.[13] In places like seventeenth-century New France, the Tridentine requirement "that the Native peoples be thoroughly catechized in their own language" would lead to "the creation of Native *dogiques* or catechists who instructed other members of their communities in their vernaculars."[14] These catechists would likely have also had some liturgical roles, though these may have varied from place to place. What the emergence of the catechist shows, however, is that despite the reification of ministry in the medieval period, there was still an openness to an authentic multiplication of ministries, at least on the local level.

Post-Vatican II Reforms

The matrix between ministry and laity established in the medieval period was significantly reformulated in the post-Vatican II period, beginning with *Sacrosanctum Concilium*, which paved the way for greater lay participation in liturgy. However, the roots of lay liturgical

13. Katharine Mahon, *Teach Us to Pray: The Lord's Prayer, Catechesis, and Ritual Reform in the Sixteenth Century* (Lanham, MD: Rowman and Littlefield, 2019). See also Maxwell E. Johnson, *The Rites of Christian Initiation: Their Evolution and Interpretation*, rev. and exp. ed. (Collegeville, MN: Liturgical Press, 2007), 366–69; Jaime Lara, "'Precious Green Jade Water': A Sixteenth-Century Adult Catechumenate in the New World," *Worship* 71 (1997): 415–28; Heliodoro Lucatero, "The Practice of Baptism in Sixteenth-Century Mexico" (PhD diss., Notre Dame, University of Notre Dame, 2007); Nathan Chase, "Baptism into Death in the Jesuit Missions in New France," *Worship* 88 (2014): 425–39.

14. Chase, "Baptism into Death," 428–29. For more, see Claudio Salvucci, *The Roman Rite in the Algonquian and Iroquoian Missions* (Merchantville, NJ: Evolution Publishing, 2008), 77–80.

ministry today find their most fertile ground in *Lumen Gentium* and *Apostolicam Actuositatem*. *Lumen Gentium* was crucial to Vatican II's theological rationale for why lay ministry was acceptable and desirable. In *Lumen Gentium*, there was an embrace of a new way of viewing the church as the people of God (10) and a new way of viewing the laity, which, as Matthew Clark notes, saw "the priestly, prophetic, and kingly dimensions of the ministry of Christ now associated with the sacrament of baptism and only secondarily with the sacrament of orders."[15] The laity, too, began to be seen as crucial to building up the church, meaning that the laity had a role to play in the liturgy, church governance, and teaching ministry. The council further affirmed the importance of the laity in the liturgy in *Apostolicam Actuositatem*. In this decree, the council stated that "the hierarchy entrusts the laity with certain tasks more closely connected with the duties of pastors: [such as] . . . certain liturgical actions" (AA 24).

While these two documents, along with *Sacrosanctum Concilium*, saw lay participation at Mass and the liturgical life of the church more broadly as vital, it would not be until Pope Paul VI issued *Ministeria Quaedam* in 1972 that the role of the laity at Mass was systematically addressed. As John Grondelski notes, "*Sacrosanctum Concilium* undertook this process of adaption in light of the Council's teachings upon the centrality of the liturgy in the Church and the Church's desire that all the faithful participate most fully in the liturgy."[16] Concerning

15. Matthew Clark, *Forward in Hope* (Notre Dame, IN: Ave Maria Press, 2009), 68.

16. John Grondelski, "Lay Ministries? A Quarter Century of *Ministeria Quaedam*," *Irish Theological Quarterly* 63 (1998): 273. For more, see also Oonagh O'Brien, "The Theology of Lay Ministry:

the historical orders of acolyte and lector, *Sacrosanctum Concilium* traded out the word "order" with "ministry" and "ordination" with "installation," and in this way was able to "declericalize these roles."[17]

While *Sacrosanctum Concilium* opened up avenues for lay liturgical ministry, it did not disconnect these newly named ministries from church control: "*Ministeria Quaedam* reserved the ministries of lector and acolyte to men . . . specified qualifications for admission to those ministries . . . and set forth certain criteria governing installation in those ministries . . . [and] retained the discipline of installing seminarians in [them] . . . during the process of priestly formation."[18] In addition to the control exerted by the hierarchy of these new lay ministries, the ministries themselves were narrowly defined. The lector, for instance, was to "proclaim the Scriptures (the Gospel excluded); read the Prayer of the Faithful; lead congregational singing; instruct the faithful, . . . prepare the 'faithful who are temporarily appointed to read the scriptures in liturgical celebrations'; and meditate upon the word." Similarly, the acolyte was to "assist the deacon and priest at mass in other liturgical celebrations; train, as need requires, 'the faithful who are temporarily appointed to assist the priest and deacon by carrying the missal, the cross or the candles or by performing other similar duties at liturgical celebration';

'Developments' Since Vatican II," *Irish Theological Quarterly* 72 (2007): 88–95; Winfried Haunerland, "The Heirs of the Clergy?: The New Pastoral Ministries and the Reform of the Minor Orders," *Worship* 75 (2001): 305–20.

17. Grondelski, "Lay Ministries?," 273.

18. Grondelski, 274.

and meditate on the Eucharist. Where circumstances require it and other canonically designated ministers are unavailable, the acolyte may also serve as an 'extraordinary minister' of the Eucharist."[19] However, the implementation of this document and its vision for a plurality of nonordained ministries was ultimately a failure. The offices of lector and acolyte were confined to men and remained steps on the way to presbyteral ordination within Catholic seminaries. In this way, *Ministeria Quaedam* failed to do what the Council of Trent had already noted was an issue: disconnecting these offices from the major orders.[20] As a result, the implementation of *Ministeria Quaedam* did little to break the medieval synthesis. This disconnection was furthered by the establishment of "extraordinary" ministers of the Eucharist in *Immensae Caritatis* in 1973.[21]

Questions were posed about *Ministeria Quaedam* by the 1987 Synod of Bishops, and Pope John Paul II issued *Christifideles Laici* in response to their questions.[22] *Christifideles Laici* is significant in its affirmation of the role of the laity in the liturgy, the church, and the world. At the same time, Hahnenberg notes, "The document appears so preoccupied with guarding the prerogatives of the ordained ministry and the special place of the hierarchical priesthood that little room is left for creatively and positively responding to . . . the new possibility for the active

19. Grondelski, 274.

20. Haunerland, "Heirs of the Clergy?," 309.

21. David N. Power, *Gifts That Differ: Lay Ministries Established and Unestablished*, Studies in the Reformed Rites of the Catholic Church 8 (New York: Pueblo Publishing, 1985), 11.

22. Grondelski, "Lay Ministries?," 275.

service of laypeople in the church."[23] Some even argue that *Christifideles Laici* resulted in a "reclericalizing" of lay ministry, something that was already underway in the way that *Ministeria Quaedam* was implemented and in the promulgation of *Immensae Caritatis*.[24]

The issue seems to be that there has not been the radical revisioning of nonordained ministry as called for by the council. Hahnenberg, in his paper, observes that this revisioning can be accomplished "by situating the ordained ministry within a broader theology of ministry in line with the Council's ecclesiological vision." Advancing lay eucharistic preaching also means challenging some inherent presuppositions within the construction and formulation of the conciliar documents. As Hahnenberg has noted for us earlier, Yves Congar, who influenced much of the ecclesiology of Vatican II, would come to see that his approach had pitted the laity against the clergy.[25] What was needed was to root all ministry again in one's baptism and, by extension, the baptized community.[26] Furthermore, taking his cue from Congar, Hahnenberg argues that the pairing "ministries-community," not "clergy-laity," is the solution to the issues we face with lay ministry today.

However, this turn to baptism (and confirmation) as the ultimate rooting of lay and ordained ministry is one

23. Hahnenberg, *Ministries*, 18.

24. Grondelski, "Lay Ministries?," 277.

25. Cf. Yves Congar, "My Path-Findings in the Theology of Laity and Ministries," *The Jurist* 32 (1972): 169–88.

26. For a helpful study that seeks to do this, see Susan K. Wood, ed., *Ordering the Baptismal Priesthood: Theologies of Lay and Ordained Ministry* (Collegeville, MN: Liturgical Press, 2003).

of two approaches. While some argue that the faithful's common baptism and confirmation give them the right to be lectors, acolytes, and eucharistic ministers, another approach holds that the laity in their liturgical ministries participate only in the orders of the church.[27] Both of these viewpoints have some precedence in the tradition, with the second being not that dissimilar from ancient concerns about the relationship between more charismatic and institutionalized ministries.

It is essential to see the distinction between these two theological viewpoints. The first sees lay liturgical ministry as stemming from the faithful's baptism. Liturgical theologians like David Power hold this view: "These two ministries [lector and acolyte] . . . are important liturgical functions . . . they are not a share in the priesthood of order, but are exercised by lay people in virtue of their share in the priesthood of Christ through baptism."[28] Power argues that the baptism of the faithful is the sole requirement for lay liturgical ministry. He sees no need for lay ministers to be commissioned or brought to participate in some way in the orders of the church. For this reason, he says that "some discipline and control may be necessary, but hardly a canonical office or a commissioning and appointment in such official form."[29]

On the other hand, the second theological view sees a need for lay liturgical ministry to be attached to some canonical office or officially sanctioned ministry that derives not from baptism but holy orders. This viewpoint holds that liturgy ministry is derived from one's participation

27. Grondelski, "Lay Ministries?," 277–78.

28. Power, *Gifts That Differ*, 5.

29. Power, 140.

in the orders of the church. As Hahnenberg notes in his discussion on *Christifideles Laici*, "While laypeople may be entrusted with certain offices and roles connected to the ministry of pastors, they do so only because of an 'official deputation given by the pastors,' exercised 'under the guidance of ecclesiastical authority.'"[30] Theologians like Grondelski contend that this is what documents like *Christifideles Laici* assert: "The demand posed by [*Christifideles Laici*] to determine whether a particular ministry [lector and acolyte] stems more properly from Orders or from Baptism and Confirmation seems *de facto* to have been made: it belongs to Orders."[31]

What is needed today is an abandonment of this latter theological perspective. The former is more in keeping with the ancient tradition of the church and the ecclesiology put forward by Vatican II. However, we would do well to keep some juridical control over these ministries. Such control can allow for the establishment of legitimate criteria for the exercise of these ministries and serve as a visible reminder of the authentic multiplicity of ministries in the church. In this way, Power's position seems too extreme. The failure to ensure the proper preparation for the ministry of lector and reader has been one of the real downfalls in implementing *Ministeria Quaedam*. Several scholars have noted that the type of preparation required for these ministries has not emerged. Furthermore, in most cases, these ministries are fulfilled by ad hoc "ministers." Nevertheless, an authentic multiplicity of ministries must primarily be rooted in the gifts of the Holy Spirit given in baptism.

30. Hahnenberg, *Ministries*, 18.

31. Grondelski, "Lay Ministries?," 277n13.

Moving Pope Francis's Vision Forward

This turn to an authentic multiplicity of ministries rooted in baptism underpins Pope Francis's treatment of lay ministry. Pope Francis has made two significant steps in *Spiritus Domini* and *Antiquum Ministerium* that can allow for an authentic multiplicity of ministries to emerge in the church today. In *Spiritus Domini*, he opened up the ministries of lector and acolyte to women while also rooting this explicitly in baptism rather than a delegation from holy orders. Unfortunately, much like *Ministeria Quaedam*, this appears to have gone unheeded in many dioceses. No concrete steps have been taken to open these ministries to men who are not in priestly formation, let alone to women! In *Antiquum Ministerium*, he instituted the role of the catechist. Here Pope Francis has tried to remind the church of the statement in *Ministeria Quaedam* that "besides the offices common to the Latin Church, there is nothing to prevent episcopal conferences from requesting others of the Apostolic See, if they judge the establishment of such offices in their region to be necessary or very useful because of special reasons."[32] Pope Francis even explicitly cited this passage from *Ministeria Quaedam* in *Antiquum Ministerium* (7).

What this reveals, and what Pope Francis's actions show, is that there is an openness to the creation of new instituted ministries that respond to the needs of the local church. One such authentic multiplication of ministries would be establishing a ministry of lay preacher.

32. International Committee on English in the Liturgy, *The Rites of the Catholic Church as Revised by Decree of the Second Vatican Ecumenical Council and Published by Authority of Pope Paul VI*, 2 vols. (New York: Pueblo Publishing, 1976), 1:728.

This lay preacher could not only take advantage of the allowances for lay preaching given in canon 766 of the 1983 Code of Canon Law but also would be allowed to preach in the context of the celebration of the Eucharist. The establishment of such a ministry and clarification of canon 767 are the only steps required. Given the importance placed on the Eucharist in the post-Vatican II period—an importance that has at times been double-edged, since it means there has often been an overemphasis on the eucharistic celebration to the detriment of the rest of the liturgical life of the church, which is also in need of revival—not to wrestle with and allow for lay preaching at the eucharistic celebration would in many ways make this a second-class ministry. The only question then becomes whether this ministry is needed in the local church and what form it would take.

I think the answer to the first is quite simple: yes, this ministry is needed and has been called for by many people in the context of the church in the United States. I would even go so far as to say that this ministry has been called for in local churches beyond the United States. It is not worth rehearsing all the scholarly and pastoral discussions on this topic,[33] but interest in greater

33. A few notable works include Nadine Foley, ed., *Preaching and the Non-Ordained: An Interdisciplinary Study* (Collegeville, MN: Liturgical Press, 1983); Mary Catherine Hilkert, "Women Preaching the Gospel," *Theology Digest* 33 (1986): 423–40; John M. Huels, "Lay Preaching," in *Disputed Questions in the Liturgy Today* (Chicago: Liturgy Training Publications, 1988), 17–26; Patrick Norris, "Lay Preaching and Canon Law: Who May Give a Homily?," *Studia Canonica* 24 (1990): 443–54; Patricia A. Parachini, *Lay Preaching: State of the Question*, American Essays in Liturgy (Collegeville, MN: Liturgical Press, 1999).

allowances for lay preaching has been frequent and sustained since Vatican II.

Preaching has not been one of the church's most robust ministries throughout history. Charlemagne, for instance, was concerned about preaching. In general, the medieval period saw the creation of homiliaries that could serve as preaching aids or even canned homilies that the homilist could give.[34] Of course, the Dominicans were also founded to address this shortfall in the ministry of the church. Preaching has always been hard, and ordained clergy are not necessarily gifted at it. But this precisely cuts to the heart of the issue. Preaching is a charism, a gift that not everyone has been given. To think that our clergy have been given this charism by virtue of their ordination is magical thinking.

Moreover, the constraints we place at present on our ordained clergy, especially that they be cisgender men, does not account for the diversity of the Body of Christ and most certainly does not allow for that diversity to be present and accounted for in the breaking open of the Word of God in our communities. In many ways, this critique has been the foundation of the work of figures like Sandra Schneiders, IHM, and Mary Catherine Hilkert, OP. Hilkert, in a response years ago to a paper on the topic by Edward Schillebeeckx, OP, cut to the heart of the matter: "We need to ask in specific pastoral situation: Who can best enflesh and proclaim the Word of God here and now—in this racial group, for these

34. For a helpful summary, see Nathan Chase, *The* Homiliae Toletanae *and the Theology of Lent and Easter*, Spicilegium Sacrum Lovaniense, Études et Documents 56, Studia Breviora 2 (Leuven: Peeters, 2020), 9–15.

women, for this group of children, etc.? What will most ensure their right and provide for their need to hear the Word of God in a way that speaks to their experience? As Professor Schillebeeckx has written in this paper, it is not a question of who is permitted to preach, but of who *can* preach? Who can best mediate the Word of God in this community situation?"[35] An office of lay preachers is an authentic multiplication of ministries in the church.

The question then is not whether this ministry should be established but how it should be implemented to ensure that those who *can* preach are prepared to share their gifts in our communities. Above all, it must be rooted in the turn to ministry as rooted in baptism and, to borrow from Congar, an understanding of ministry that is not based on a "clergy-laity" distinction, but one of "ministries-community." In the end, the establishment of such an office of lay preachers on those grounds would contribute not only to preaching in the United States and abroad but to a more theologically and ecclesiologically healthy understanding of ministry that might allow for other authentic ministries to become authorized—like pastoral assistants or *delegados de la palabra*[36]—and also to enable other ministries to spring forth. For the harvest is plentiful *and so too are the laborers,* if we look beyond our narrow understanding of ministry.

35. Foley, *Preaching and the Non-Ordained*, 53.

36. Haunerland, "Heirs of the Clergy?," 313–16.

Toward an Inclusive Model of Eucharistic Preaching in the Catholic Church

Mary Erika N. Bolaños

Dr. Edward Hahnenberg made clear points about the Catholic Church's stance on lay preaching, presenting a theological and ecclesiological discourse. His analysis resonates with the ecclesiological advancements of the Second Vatican Council and subsequent theological inquiries on the nature and structure of ministry in the church. He has made a particularly thought-provoking observation with his examination of lay eucharistic preaching, framing it within the dichotomy of "authentic" and "inauthentic" expressions of ministry diversification. This dialectical exploration invites further investigation, especially in the context of Francis A. Sullivan's seminal work, *Charisms and Charismatic Renewal: A Biblical and Theological Study*, which offers profound insights into the role of charisms within the church's ministry framework.[1]

1. Francis A. Sullivan, *Charisms and Charismatic Renewal: A Biblical and Theological Study* (Eugene, OR: Wipf & Stock, 1984).

Indeed, the nuances of canonical concerns are paramount, particularly in the distinction drawn between canon 766, which allows for lay preaching under specified conditions, and canon 767 §1, which explicitly reserves the homily to ordained ministers. These distinctions raise profound ecclesiological inquiries regarding the essence of preaching and its integration within the liturgical celebration. The homily, as an intrinsic component of the Liturgy of the Word, serves the purpose of expounding upon the scriptural passages and their relevance to the lives of the faithful. In this context, the theological argument for lay preaching encounters significant ecclesiological and liturgical boundaries.

Yet in light of the evolving ecclesiology of Vatican II and the subsequent calls for a more synodal and participatory church, as articulated in Pope Francis's apostolic exhortation *Evangelii Gaudium*, it becomes imperative to reassess these boundaries. The pope's emphasis on the "art of accompaniment" and the recognition of everyone's ability to be "artisans of their destiny"[2] prompt a reevaluation of how the church discerns and affirms ministries within its community. This reevaluation includes consideration of diverse and enriching perspectives offered by lay theologians and preachers such as Phyllis Zagano,[3]

2. Pope Francis, Apostolic Exhortation *Evangelii Gaudium* ("On the Proclamation of the Gospel in Today's World") (November 24, 2013) 169–93.

3. Phyllis Zagano, *Women Deacons: Past, Present, Future* (New York: Paulist Press, 2011). Zagano argues for the inclusion of laypersons in preaching to reflect the Church's diversity more fully. Zagano's work highlights the historical precedent and contemporary need for diverse ministerial voices, including women's voices.

Gloria Ulterino,[4] Sherry Weddell,[5] and, within the Philippine context, Bo Sanchez. These voices bring unique insights and experiences contributing to the church's mission and vitality in the modern world.

Allow me to share my point using the context of my country. I am from the Philippines—a country with a Catholic population of 79.5 percent. Unsurprisingly, the latest study on nominal and lapsed Catholics in the Philippines shows a significant decrease in the number of Catholics practicing their faith. Fr. Jason Laguerta, the head of the Institute for Research and Development of the Archdiocese of Manila, spearheaded the study and presented the results during the Fifth General Assembly of the World Catholic Association for Communication's SIGNIS Philippines on July 15, 2023.[6] While Catholicism remains dominant, the percentage of active members from other religious groups is more noteworthy. The study shows that most Catholics lack the component of witnessing their faith in their lives. He recommends that

4. As a preacher, author, and founding member of Women of the Well, Gloria Ulterino from the Diocesan Office of Women in Rochester, New York, started preaching in 1986, a time when the United States bishops had established norms for lay preachers, and Vatican II had opened up possibilities for such.

5. Sherry A. Weddell, *Forming Intentional Disciples: The Path to Knowing and Following Jesus*, 2nd rev. ed. (Huntington, IN: Our Sunday Visitor, 2022). Weddell discusses the critical role of lay Christians in witnessing to the faith, arguing that laypeople, through their authentic witness and articulation of personal faith stories, are pivotal in the new evangelization.

6. RVA News, "Significant Decrease in Number of Practicing Catholics in Philippines," *Sunday Examiner*, July 28, 2023, https://www.examiner.org.hk/2023/07/28/significant-decrease-in-number-of-practicing-catholics-in-philippines/news.

the church delve deep into the grassroots level to be fully present and connect with the people.

Bo Sanchez, a lay Catholic preacher and founder of the Light of Jesus—the Feast Service, echoed these concerns. His initiative, the Feast, began in the early 2000s as a Sunday prayer gathering accompanied by Holy Mass, where Sanchez and his team of "Feast Builders" preach. Over the years, the Feast has expanded internationally, establishing prayer groups in regions across Asia, the United States, the United Kingdom, Oceania, and Canada. His approach provides a model for revitalizing faith communities, particularly among the youth and their families, through relatable and experiential preaching. His ability to draw individuals back to the sacraments and foster a spirit of community service underscores the significance of authentic and relatable ministry in addressing contemporary challenges within the church.

In an interview conducted by Cardinal Luis Antonio Tagle, Sanchez shared insights on the foremost challenges confronting young people regarding evangelization. He emphasized that youths yearn for an authentic and nurturing church environment. Central to this longing is the need for genuine individuals who embody and convey God's love. Sanchez emphasized the importance of personal relationships in experiencing and understanding God's love, asserting that theoretical knowledge alone cannot suffice.[7]

7. CBCP News, "Heart to Heart Talk with Cardinal Chito" segment of the 2019 Philippine Conference on the New Evangelization at the University of Santo Tomas Pavilion in Manila, July 19, 2019, https://cbcpnews.net/cbcpnews/young-people-looking-for-authentic-witnesses-says-bo-sanchez.

Building on these observations and anchoring them to some of the points mentioned by Dr. Hahnenberg, the theological justification for broadening the commissioning of qualified lay preachers for eucharistic preaching rests on several pillars:

1. *Baptismal priesthood:* All the baptized share in Christ's priesthood, prophetic, and royal mission. This shared priesthood forms the basis for a more inclusive understanding of ministry within the church (*Lumen Gentium* [LG] 10). Vatican II, on one side, emphasizes "a true equality with regard to the dignity and the activity which [all the faithful] share in the building up of the body of Christ" (LG 32); on the other, it ambiguously declares that "the term laity is here understood to mean all the faithful *except* those in holy Orders and those who belong to a religious state approved by the church" (LG 31; emphasis added).

2. *Diversity of charisms:* There is no monopoly of gifts. The Spirit's distribution of gifts for the common good includes the gift of preaching, which is not limited to the ordained (1 Cor 12:7-10). Building on conciliar foundations (*Lumen Gentium* and *Apostolicam Actuositatem*), the theological rationale for expanding lay preaching emerges from the recognition of the diversity of gifts (charisms) bestowed by the Holy Spirit upon the members of the church for the common good (1 Cor 12:4-11). Theologians like Edward Schillebeeckx and Yves Congar have argued that these gifts, including the gift of preaching, are not confined to the ordained but are distributed among the faithful for the edification of the church and fulfilling its mission.

3. *Liturgical and pastoral adaptability:* The church's liturgical laws, while safeguarding the sacredness of

worship, also allow for pastoral adaptability in response to the needs of the faithful and the broader mission of evangelization (*Sacrosanctum Concilium* [SC] 37–40). The "Constitution on the Sacred Liturgy" proposed to "impart an ever-increasing vigor to the Christian lives of the faithful; to adapt more closely to the needs of our age those institutions which are subject to change," to promote unity among Christians; and to invite others into this life (SC 1). We all know that baptism is the key, unlocking the door to full participation; indeed, Christ is present in the entire worshiping Church, as well as in the priest, the Eucharist, and the Word of God (SC 7). Therefore, "it is very much the wish of the church that all the faithful should be led to take that full, conscious, and active part in liturgical celebrations," to which the baptized "have a right and to which they are bound by reason of their Baptism" (SC 14). Should it not include lay preaching?

The Catholic Church is open to new challenges and must not refuse to recognize the "signs of the times" in which the will of God shows itself. The concept of discerning these signs was introduced by Vatican II, highlighting the church's responsibility to interpret contemporary realities in light of the Gospel. *Gaudium et Spes* says: "The church carries the responsibility of reading the signs of the times and of interpreting them in the light of the Gospel, if it is to carry out its task. In language intelligible to every generation, it should be able to answer the ever recurring questions which people ask about the meaning of this present life and of the life to come, and how one is related to the other. We must be aware of and understand the aspirations, the yearnings, and the often dramatic features of the world in which we live" (4).

Furthermore, the historical roots of our canonical practices underscore their evolution over time. An illustrative example is found in the life of Origen, a church father who dedicated his life to Christian teaching and preaching with remarkable missionary zeal. Renowned for his eloquence, theological depth, and charismatic delivery, Origen earned widespread recognition and respect across the Roman Empire, not only as a preacher but also as a theologian of significant stature. In the 230s, bishops Theoktistos of Caesarea Maritima and Alexander of Jerusalem, recognizing his gifts and contributions, extended him the rare commission to preach during the eucharistic celebration on Sundays—a privilege typically reserved for ordained priests—even though Origen himself had not received ordination. This historical account, as documented by Eusebius of Caesarea in his *Ecclesiastical History*,[8] underscores the flexibility and adaptability of ecclesiastical practices to accommodate extraordinary contributions to the faith, even in its early stages.

8. Eusebius, *Historia Ecclesiastica*, VI, 19,16.

Synodal Church

Eucharistic Preaching in a Synodal Church

Layla A. Karst

Our symposium, "The Pastoral Charge for Lay Catholic Eucharistic Preaching," has charged us with the following question: Can a theological case be made for the church to charge or commission a more extensive and diverse pool of qualified lay preachers and evangelists to preach the Word of God at the Eucharist? I join my voice to the chorus of scholars and ministers who have answered this question in the affirmative. Yes, I believe the church *can* and *should* permit and commission lay preachers to preach at the Eucharist at the moment of the homily.

My aim in this essay is to reflect on this question liturgically while keeping in mind that questions and tensions about the liturgy are always at their root questions and contentions about the church. That is, liturgical questions are always also ecclesiological questions. As a scholar who positions herself in liturgical theology, I find myself returning time and again to Aidan Kavanagh's claim that in the liturgy, the church is "caught in the act of being most overtly itself."[1] Indeed, the church's

1. Aidan Kavanagh, *On Liturgical Theology* (Collegeville, MN: Liturgical Press, 1984), 75.

liturgies are enacted ecclesiologies—sites where the theologically curious can discover the nature of the church in that particular time and place, in and through their liturgical ways of proceeding.[2] In this movement, liturgical practice functions as an enacted *sensus fidei*, affirming the community's shared beliefs and even giving rise to new theologies that are eventually accepted as doctrines and practices that are ultimately supposed to be normative: *lex orandi, lex credendi.*

But in the life of the church, the interplay between liturgy and theology is more fluid and dynamic than our abbreviation of Prosper of Aquitaine's classic axiom might suggest. Liturgical practice has also been *responsive* to changing theological expressions, understandings, and commitments. The liturgical reforms of the Second Vatican Council are evidence enough of this liturgical dynamism where, for example, *Sacrosanctum Concilium*'s insistence on the full, conscious, and active participation of the entire assembly becomes inseparable from *Lumen Gentium*'s ecclesiology of the people of God—both of which are the culmination of liturgical and ecclesiological developments that long preceded the council and only eventually found in the conciliar texts a magisterial affirmation and embrace. Liturgical reform is typically undertaken when liturgical practice is out of sync with current theological commitments, when the church's *enacted* ecclesiology is inconsistent with its *professed* ecclesiology. And liturgical debates are often waged in the service of competing ecclesiologies.

The real wisdom of Prosper's axiom is to remind us that neither our liturgical practices nor our ecclesiology

2. Kavanagh, *On Liturgical Theology*, 67.

have ever been fixed in stone to be re-chiseled only occasionally in the hallowed halls of ecumenical councils. They have always fluctuated with the faith communities' theological convictions, which give them expression and life. Sometimes, the liturgy runs out ahead of our theological imagination—*lex orandi, lex credendi*—but other times, shifting theological understandings critique and reshape our liturgical celebrations to give fuller expression to the faith of the church—*lex credendi, lex orandi*. As a liturgical theologian, I feel much more at home in analyzing and reflecting on the theologies that arise from the church's diverse, lived liturgical celebrations. By examining the nature and function of the homily within the current Roman Rite, we can ask: Does the current restriction of the homily to the ordained make sense within the ritual logic of the eucharistic liturgy?

But this approach alone seems insufficient in light of another question that has been tugging at me, as perhaps it has been tugging at so many of us theologians, faith leaders, ministers lay and ordained, and any who bear some vocational responsibility to and for our ecclesial institutions: What kind of claim and consequence does Pope Francis's emerging synodal ecclesiology have on our liturgical practice? Under Francis's leadership, Vatican II's people of God and pilgrim ecclesiologies have found new life and new interpretations in the church's ongoing discussions, experiences, and reflections on synodality. This new understanding of what it means to be and proceed as church has implications for how we enact and embody this church in and through our liturgical practice. The second part of this essay asks what eucharistic preaching should look like in a synodal church.

Thinking Liturgically: Some Notes on the Homily

The Homily in the Liturgical Reforms of Vatican II

Preaching was not considered integral to the eucharistic liturgy in the decades leading up to the Second Vatican Council. In the preconciliar liturgical books, preaching during this liturgy was an option—recommended, certainly, but also easily omitted for various pastoral concerns. For some liturgists, preaching was accidental to the liturgy, and a few even considered it an "interruption" to the action of the Mass.[3] I am sympathetic with these perspectives, given the typical form preaching during the liturgy often took when it did happen. The historian William O'Shea describes preaching in the decades before the council as "a thinly-disguised classroom lecture" that was thoroughly unrelated to the liturgical moment or celebration.[4] Vatican II's restoration of the homily as the normative form for eucharistic preaching was more than a return to biblical preaching, as laudable as that is. It was also a restoration of preaching as a constitutive element of the eucharistic liturgy itself.[5] As such, in the promulgation of the 1969 Roman Missal, preaching at the Sunday Eucharist was no longer

3. Robert Waznak, *An Introduction to the Homily* (Collegeville, MN: Liturgical Press, 1998), vii.

4. William O'Shea, "The Sermon Is Part of the Mass," *The Homiletic and Pastoral Review* (March 1960): 517–26.

5. *Sacrosanctum Concilium* ("Constitution on the Sacred Liturgy" [SC]) 35, 52. This harkens back to an early patristic understanding of the homily. For example, Origen described the liturgical homily as a "mutual search by preacher and congregation—a seeking after the voice of God." In Thomas Carroll, *Preaching the Word*, Message of the Fathers of the Church, vol. 11 (Wilmington, DE: Michael Glazier, 1984), 43.

optional. Preaching—not any form of preaching, but a *homily*—is required, or at least it can be omitted only for serious reasons![6]

The regular inclusion of the homily within the church's eucharistic liturgy was an innovation compared to the rite that most Catholics had known for the previous four hundred years. It accompanied other seeming innovations, which included the opening of several liturgical ministries to laymen and eventually laywomen, as well as the encouragement of fuller and more active participation by the entire assembly, who were also empowered toward a more active sharing of the church's mission of proclamation and evangelization outside of the liturgy.[7] At the council, the Eucharist became a liturgy *of* the people of God rather than one the priest celebrated on their behalf.

Perhaps it is not surprising that the minister of the homily was, for many years following the council, a contested issue. The 1973 publication of the *Directory for Masses with Children* included its liturgical innovation when it permitted laypeople to speak to children during the moment of the homily if the priest found it too difficult to do so.[8] That same year, the bishops of West Germany received authorization to commission certain members of the laity to preach and even give

6. See SC 52 and GIRM 66.

7. See *Lumen Gentium* 32; *Gaudium et Spes* 43; *Apostolicam Actuositatem* ("Decree on the Apostolate of Lay People") 6 and 10; and canons 208, 211, and 230.

8. Congregation for Divine Worship, *Directory for Masses with Children* (Washington, DC: United States Catholic Conference, 1974).

homilies when necessary.[9] The 1983 Code of Canon Law permitted lay preaching at times and places where it was previously prohibited (c. 766). It affirmed that the laity can be called to cooperate with priests or bishops in their ministry of the Word (c. 761). At the same time, the code restricted the eucharistic homily to the ordained (c. 767). The 1983 Code of Canon Law opened a dynamic and robust conversation about lay eucharistic preaching in the theological academy, and an increase in the practice of lay eucharistic preaching was observed, especially in universities and monasteries, but also in several parishes.[10]

Beginning in the 1990s, a series of Vatican instructions expressed increasing notes of alarm about perceived confusion about the role of the priest given the expansion of ministerial roles undertaken by the laity, including as preachers (*lex orandi, lex credendi*). The 1997 instruction *Ecclesia de Mysterio* reinscribed preaching in the sacrament of orders rather than baptism, ensuring that lay preaching is not confused with or held on par with preaching by the ordained.[11] Subsequent instructions

9. See International Committee on English in the Liturgy, *Documents on the Liturgy, 1963–1979: Conciliar, Papal, and Curial Texts* (Collegeville, MN: Liturgical Press, 1982), 344.

10. The Dominicans were at the forefront of this effort in the US academy, including their organization of a special interdisciplinary conference on preaching by the nonordained in Columbus, Ohio, in 1982. The papers presented at this conference are available in Nadine Foley's edited volume *Preaching and the Non-Ordained: An Interdisciplinary Study* (Collegeville, MN: Liturgical Press, 1983).

11. The 1997 *Ecclesiae de Mysterio* ("Instruction on Certain Questions Regarding the Collaboration of the Non-Ordained Faithful in the Sacred Ministry of Priest") allows that laity may be admitted to

by the Vatican congregation and individual episcopal conferences emphasized that lay preaching was to be always the exception and never the norm. They focused specifically on limiting the parameters for lay preaching during the Eucharist, prescribing that lay preaching is permissible provided it occurs at a time other than the homily[12] or, eventually, outside of the Mass entirely.[13] This magisterial preoccupation with the minister of the homily created further ambiguity about the nature of the homily itself.

Understanding the Homily: Ministerial and Liturgical Definitions

What is the nature and function of the homily in the eucharistic celebration? The most restrictive definitions of the homily have suggested, as Robert Waznak

---

preach, but emphasizes that there is no *right or faculty* to preach for laypeople, as there is for the ordained. "This exclusion is not based on the preaching ability of sacred ministers nor their theological preparation, but on that function which is reserved to them in virtue of having received the Sacrament of Holy Orders" (3.1). Rather, lay preaching is to be considered always and only as an exceptional practice and permissible only in the absence of a suitable ordained preacher. Elissa Rinere notes that John Paul II's endorsement of this instruction raises it to the status of legislation, an unusual status for this sort of instruction to attain. See also Elissa Rinere, CP, "Lay Preaching: By Whose Authority?," *Preach* (May/June 2006): 25–30.

12. "USCCB Decree Implementing Canon 766 of the Code of Canon Law," USCCB Committee on the Liturgy Newsletter XXXVII (December 13, 2001).

13. Congregation for Divine Worship and the Discipline of the Sacraments, *Redemptionis Sacramentum,* "Instruction on Certain Matters to Be Observed or to Be Avoided Regarding the Most Holy Eucharist" (March 25, 2004).

does, for example, in his *Introduction to the Homily*, that a homily is *by definition* (that is, "by constitutive law") "a form of preaching which can [only] be done by a priest or a deacon."[14] Thus, he notes that while lay preaching can be included in liturgical celebrations, this preaching (not unlike preconciliar clerical preaching at the Eucharist) is optional or accidental to the liturgical action and thus correctly referred to not as a homily, but rather as an "explanation of the readings" or "a personal reflection" or "speaking after the gospel."[15] This nominalism has produced some familiar if questionable liturgical practices where lay preaching is preceded by a proverbial wink and nod of the presiding minister who either preaches briefly himself before ceding the pulpit to ensure the priority of the priestly word over the lay one or welcomes the lay preacher by overenunciating the invitation to offer a "*personal reflection* on the readings of the day," insisting, or at least insinuating, that whatever is about to happen not be misunderstood as a liturgical or ecclesial action on par with ordained preaching.

This liturgical nominalism serves a not-so-subtle clericalism that reinforces the priority of clerical preaching over lay preaching by simultaneously declaring eucharistic preaching the "highest" form of preaching in the church and subsequently (or perhaps therefore) reserving this form of preaching (and only this form of preaching) exclusively to the ordained, not by virtue

14. Waznak, *Introduction to the Homily*, 135.

15. The 1997 instruction *Ecclesia de Mysterio* follows this logic to a point when it allows that laypersons can provide "instruction" or "testimonies" during eucharistic liturgies provided they are not confused with the homily (3.2).

of their liturgical function of presidency but because of their ordained state.[16] This nominalism also risks an excessive juridicalism, whereby the homily is defined by the canons of the code rather than by the liturgical rites and texts. Canonist James Coriden points out that "none of the [liturgical] source documents define the homily in terms of who preaches it."[17] Even the text of canon 767, which restricts the homily to the ordained, does not support this nominalist definition. Instead, this canonical restriction is justified by the homily's *liturgical character*, which is somewhat perplexing in its own right. This explanation makes sense in a preconciliar rite, which reserved all liturgical actions to the clergy. But in the postconciliar liturgy, where the entire people of God are invited to full participation, albeit in distinct and ordered ways, the liturgical character of the homily does not on its own serve as sufficient justification for a *constitutive* restriction of the homily to the ordained. If this were the case, we might conclude that *only* those actions reserved to the deacon or priest can be properly considered "liturgical" or "constitutive of the liturgical celebration." Thus, the proclamation of the Gospel is constitutive of the liturgy, while the other readings are not. Or the eucharistic prayer is liturgical while the distribution (and reception)

16. This is the explicit logic of *Ecclesia de Mysterio*, which interprets *Dei Verbum*'s claim that among pastoral preaching, catechesis, and all forms of Christian instruction, the homily holds pride of place in light of the unique right and faculty of the ordained to preach it. *Ecclesia de Mysterio* 3.1, and *Dei Verbum* 24.

17. James A. Coriden, *New Commentary on the Code of Canon Law*, ed. John P. Beal, James A. Coriden, and Thomas J. Green (New York: Paulist Press, 2000), 929–30.

of communion is not.[18] Even *Ecclesia de Mysterio* does not restrict the definition of the "homily," allowing laypersons to preach homilies in non-eucharistic liturgies, suggesting that the term *homily* can be understood as liturgical preaching, but not necessarily restricted to eucharistic preaching.[19]

Understanding the homily as liturgical preaching points us toward different criteria for determining the appropriate minister. The ritual logic—the homily's specific liturgical context and function—suggests who may preach it. We can see this operative definition when the case for restricting the eucharistic homily to the ordained is made based on the value and priority of ritual continuity between Word and table, with a single minister presiding over both.[20] Here, the homily is broadly defined as a *liturgical* action, specifically a *presidential* action. Lay homilies are deemed inappropriate where the presidential action is restricted to the ordained, as is the case with the eucharistic liturgy. A lay-preached homily is also appropriate in non-eucharistic liturgies where the laity can be authorized to preside.

While this definition is tidy, this reasoning seems to be deployed only when the question of *lay* preaching is at stake and has little basis in current liturgical texts or practice. The *General Instruction of the Roman Missal* explicates the *presidential elements* of the eucharistic lit-

18. The *General Instruction of the Roman Missal*, in 98–107, explicitly treats the particular liturgical functions of the nonordained.

19. *Ecclesia de Mysterio* 3.4.

20. Coriden, *New Commentary on the Code*, 929. See also United States Conference of Catholic Bishops, *Preaching the Mystery of Faith: The Sunday Homily* (Washington, DC: USCCB, 2012), 17.

urgy: the eucharistic prayer, orations, and the final blessing, as well as informal instructions, introductions, or explanatory comments for the benefit of the assembly (30–31). Notably absent from these presidential articles is any mention of the homily, described more broadly as part of the proclamation of the Word of God, implying that the proclamation of the Word of God, including the homily, is ministerial, not presidential. While the normative liturgical practice may be for the one presiding at the table of the Eucharist to also preside at the table of the Word, frequent exceptions are made when another ordained minister does the preaching—whether they are concelebrating or not—without any apparent confusion about the relationship between the two.[21] Thus, the continuity provided between Word and table is not that of a single presiding minister but rather the continuity of an indistinguishable clerical presidency between the two. Even if we prioritize the need for a ritual and presidential continuity between the table of the Word and the table of the Eucharist, we should be cautious of the presumption that the ordained are the only ritual symbols and guarantors of this unity. Instead, the ritual action itself expresses and maintains this continuity.

21. According to the *General Instruction of the Roman Missal*, the homily should ordinarily be given by the priest who is presiding at the liturgy, although it may be entrusted to a concelebrating priest or deacon, or to a bishop or priest present at the celebration even if they are not concelebrating (but never a layperson). See 65. It is notable that Pope Francis does treat the homily as a presidential action in his apostolic letter "On the Liturgical Formation of the People of God" (*Desiderio Desideravi*) (June 29, 2022) 55, although the same explicitness is missing in *Evangelii Gaudium*.

Consider the continuity of ritual action between the Liturgy of the Eucharist and the Liturgy of the Word. During the Liturgy of the Eucharist, the priest offers the eucharistic prayer with the assent of the full assembly. The eucharistic prayer, at least in the West, reaches its climax in the institution narrative, where the priest acts most overtly *in persona Christi* as he repeats the words of Jesus. Once the prayer concludes, the action shifts from the priest to the full assembly, who respond in prayer, exchanging a sign of peace, and communion—the encounter between Christ and the people of God, wherein the sacrament of the altar becomes incarnated in the concrete and unique community assembled in that particular time and place. While the eucharistic prayer is always restricted to the ordained, the laity are authorized, when need and prudence dictate (which is almost always!) to serve as ministers of communion.

During the Liturgy of the Word, the *General Instruction of the Roman Missal* describes the proclamation of the Gospel (and not the homily) as the "high point" of the rite (60). It is here that both ritual and tradition confess that Christ is present and speaking to the congregation, perhaps suggesting that in the eucharistic liturgy, the proclamation of the Gospel be reserved to the ordained minister who serves a particular symbolic function in the ritual action, standing *in persona Christi*.[22] What remains more ambiguous in the liturgical rite

22. Vatican II's "Decree on the Ministry and Life of Priests" (*Presbyterorum Ordinis*) likewise links the two tables through the priestly proclamation of the Gospel and the spiritual offering of the Eucharist, but curiously the *General Instruction of the Roman Missal* is explicit that the Gospel be proclaimed "by the Deacon or, in his absence, by another Priest" unless the celebrant is the only

is the function of the homily. The current rite follows the canonical restriction of the homily to the ordained minister. Still, the liturgical action suggests that the homily is ritually closer to the communion rite than to the eucharistic prayer. During the homily, the Word of God proclaimed in the assembly is "broken open," as the saying goes; it becomes particular; it is verbally incarnated in and through preaching. The homily is an unrepeatable liturgical action that is defined not only by its minister but also by its hearers; and, like the rite of Communion, it is unique to its own particular time and place.[23] The homily, understood within the ritual context of the liturgy, is not fundamentally a *priestly* or *presidential* action—it is a ritual act of communion. As such, a concern for ritual and ministerial continuity between the two tables suggests that the minister of the Word of God may suitably be drawn from both the lay and ordained members of the assembly.

A liturgical understanding of the homily as a place of encounter and communion is consistent with how Pope Francis writes about the homily in *Evangelii Gaudium*.[24] Francis describes the homily as a liturgical and "quasi-sacramental" (142) action that makes an already ongoing

---

ordained minister present. The GIRM ritually links the two tables through the proclamation of the homily, which should normally be preached by the one who presides at the altar of the Eucharist. See *Presbyterorum Ordinis* 2, and GIRM 59 and 65.

23. I have in mind here especially Mary Catherine Hilkert, who lifts up the active role of the listener in the preaching event. Mary Catherine Hilkert, *Naming Grace: Preaching and the Sacramental Imagination,* (New York: Continuum, 1997), 84.

24. Pope Francis, Apostolic Exhortation *Evangelii Gaudium* ("On the Proclamation of the Gospel in Today's World") (November 24, 2013).

dialogue between God and God's people visible and concrete and guides both assembly and preacher to a "life-changing communion with Christ" (138). Although Francis presumes in this text that the minister of the eucharistic homily is ordained, curiously, the image Francis offers the church of the eucharistic preacher is not one of an apostle or a priest or even Christ himself but that of a mother speaking to her child (139). Francis writes that a mother's authority when she preaches comes not because of her position in the family or some ontological authority she holds as a mother but rather because her children know they are loved. More than a simple metaphor for priestly authority, Francis's choice of image suggests that the preacher's authority, even during the eucharistic liturgy, stems not from sacramental ordination but from their loving service to the people of God. That a laywoman can exemplify this homiletic authority but is currently restricted from offering the homily herself should give us pause.

Thinking Synodally: Some Notes on the People of God

While our current liturgical rite invites us to reconsider restricting the homily to the ordained, liturgical reform should also be informed by ongoing theological reflection on the nature of the church itself. In September 2021, Pope Francis convened the entire church of God in synod, inviting Catholics to reflect on ways of being and proceeding as church in the twenty-first century.[25]

25. Secretary General of the Synod of Bishops, "Preparatory Document" (Vatican City, September 2021), 1.

Pope Francis has frequently described synodality as the work of "journeying together," a phrase that may speak more richly and provocatively to the heart than to the mind! As Rafael Luciani has observed, synodality is a reception of Vatican II that, from among the many ecclesiologies expressed in the documents of the council, situates the ecclesial image of the people of God as the normative or foundational theological understanding of the church.[26] At the same time, Francis's vision of synodality is fundamentally pneumatological, balancing the Christocentric vision of the council with one that is thoroughly Spirit-forward. Nathalie Becquart, XMCJ, undersecretary to the Synod of Bishops, writes that synodality "invites us to see and experience the church as a people of missionary pilgrims" in which all are called to a shared co-responsibility, rooted in baptism and animated by the Holy Spirit, to the proclamation of the Gospel throughout the world.[27] There are three dimensions of synodality that I find particularly relevant to the question of lay eucharistic preaching:

1. *Listening*: Almost every summary or discussion of synodality insists that a synodal church is a listening church. Pope Francis described this as "a mutual listening in which everyone has something to learn. The faithful people, the college of bishops, the Bishop of Rome:

26. International Theological Commission, *Synodality in the Life and Mission of the Church* (March 2, 2018), 42. Rafael Luciani, *Synodality: A New Way of Proceeding in the Church*, trans. Joseph Owens, SJ (New York: Paulist Press, 2022), 2.

27. Nathalie Becquart, "Synodality According to Pope Francis: A Call from God, an Open Path, a Moving Thought," in *Walking Together: The Way of Synodality*, ed. General Secretariat of the Synod (Maryknoll, NY: Orbis Books, 2023), xiv.

all listening to each other, and all listening to the Holy Spirit, the Spirit of Truth."[28] This co-responsibility for listening among all the people of God has its corollary in the co-responsibility for what Francis has described as missionary *parrhesia*.

2. *Parrhesia*: Although less prominent in general ecclesial texts on synodality, Pope Francis has spoken consistently about the need for boldness or frankness of speech constituting the synodal style.[29] While this desire for bold speech certainly applies to all consultative processes that are part of the ongoing synod, for Francis, *parrhesia* is connected fundamentally to the practice of preaching.[30] In the Acts of the Apostles, *parrhesia* describes the style of early Christian preachers: frank, bold, and indicative of the inner freedom that arises from a sense of one's own dignity in Christ, one's belonging to the ecclesial community, and one's co-responsibility for the work at hand.[31] To use a phrase for which I am indebted to our

28. Pope Francis, "Address on the Fiftieth Anniversary of the Institution of the Synod of Bishops" (October 17, 2015). See also Francis, opening speech of the 2014 Family Synod (October 6, 2014).

29. See Pope Francis, "Address at the Opening of the Seventieth General Assembly of the Italian Episcopal Conference" (May 22, 2017); Francis, "Address to the Congregation of Bishops" (February 27, 2014); and International Theological Commission, *Synodality in the Life and Mission*, 120–21.

30. Pope Francis, "The Gift of the Holy Spirit: Frankness, Courage, Parresia," homily (April 18, 2020), https://www.vatican.va/content/francesco/en/cotidie/2020/documents/papa-francesco-cotidie_20200418_lafranchezza-dellapredicazione.html.

31. Arco den Heijer, "The Performance of *Parrhesia* in Philo and Acts," *Journal for the Study of the New Testament* 45, no. 2 (December 2022).

colleague Ed Hahnenberg, *parrhesia* is preaching with a sense of "ecclesial agency,"[32] preaching authorized by the Spirit, and the Spirit manifests in its proclamation.

3. *Dialogue*: This dynamic interplay between listening and speaking is dialogical. It presumes distinction and difference between members of the people of God, not only between the lay and ordained! Francis frequently speaks of the need for dialogue between bishops and the rest of the people of God, but he also speaks of the need for dialogue between the young and the old and between the rich and the poor. In these cases, Francis preaches and teaches a reversal of our usual way of doing things. The bishops are exhorted to listen and the laity to speak.[33] The young are encouraged to lift their voices even as they must also learn to listen to the wisdom of their elders.[34] The rich are invited to listen to the witness and proclamation of the poor, called a *locus theologicus*.[35] Francis's vision of a synodal church does not collapse distinction, even among ordained and lay, but neither does it define that distinction by who gets to speak and who gets to listen. In a synodal church, all the baptized are called to be both teachers and disciples.[36]

32. For a robust discussion of "ecclesial agency," see also Graham McDonough, "What Is Assumed about a Catholic Student's Ecclesial Agency, and Why It Matters to Catholic Schooling," *Journal of Catholic Education* 14, no. 3 (March 2011): 272–91.

33. Francis, "Address on the Fiftieth Anniversary of the Institution of the Synod of Bishops" (October 17, 2015).

34. Pope Francis, "Prayer Vigil in Preparation of World Youth Day" (April 8, 2017).

35. Francis, *Evangelii Gaudium* 126.

36. Pope Francis, Apostolic Constitution *Episcopalis Communio* (September 15, 2018).

If a distinction characterizes ministry (and authority) in a synodal church, the distinction is one of service—service to the Word of God and the people of God. In his 2018 apostolic constitution *Episcopalis Communio*, which reformed the Synod of Bishops, Francis instituted three prominent reforms. First, he made episcopal consultation with the people of God a mandatory part of every synodal process. Thus, the Synod of Bishops was not meant simply to address and respond to perceived issues and challenges within the people of God. Now, the bishops must also serve as servants and stewards of the wisdom and voice of the people of God. Second, this shift roots the teaching authority of the Synod of Bishops not in the magisterial authority of the ordained but first and foremost in the *sensus fidei*, and thus allows for the promulgation of synodal texts as authentic and authoritative teachings of the church, rather than reducing the Synod of Bishops to the simple consultative body that it was under previous papacies. Finally, while the ordinary members of the Synod of Bishops are, in fact, still bishops, Francis opened the door for the inclusion and full participation, even as voting members, by non-bishops, including the laity, elevating the role and voice of the laity (as well as priests and deacons) where they were previously restricted. Again, Francis's reforms do not collapse the distinction between lay and ordained, but they reconstitute their relationship.

In more recent documents from Francis and the synod itself, this synodal way has emerged in marked contrast to another way of proceeding with which the church today is intimately familiar: the way of clericalism. Luciani has argued (persuasively, in my opinion) that this clericalist institutional model constitutes the fundamental ecclesial failure of our time.[37] Concern about this isolation and elevation of the clergy from laypeople in pyramidal systems of authoritarian power frequently appears, for example, in synodal syntheses and preparatory texts, including in concerns about liturgies that excessively center the celebrant, disempower the assembly, and isolate the clergy from the laity.[38] The *Instrumentum Laboris* for the gathering of the synod in Rome in October 2023 asked participants to consider this problem of clericalism in two different ways, asking (1) "Can we discern together how a clerical mindset, whether in Clergy or Laity, inhibits the full expression of both the vocation of ordained Ministries in the Church as well as that of other members of the People of God? How can we find ways to overcome this together?" and (2) "What forms of clericalism persist in the Christian community? A perception of distance between the lay Faithful and their Pastors persists: what can help to overcome it? What forms of exercising authority and responsibility should be superseded as they are not appropriate for a properly constituted synodal Church?" In raising calls for reform, the recent synod assembly invites the church to consider how our eucharistic liturgies might

37. Luciani, *Synodality*, 7–14.

38. General Secretariat of the Synod, XVI Ordinary General Assembly of the Synod of Bishops, "'Enlarge the Space of Your Tent' (Is 54:2): Working Document for the Continental Stage" (October 2022) 33, 58, 93; XVI Ordinary General Assembly of the Synod of Bishops, *Instrumentum Laboris* for the Second Session, "*How* to Be a Missionary Synodal Church" (October 2024), B2.4 and B3.1; and XVI Ordinary General Assembly of the Synod of Bishops, Synthesis Report for the First Session, "A Synodal Church in Mission" (October 4–29, 2023), 11c.

better embrace a more synodal style of celebration and become more credible manifestations of the synodal church.[39]

Eucharistic Preaching in a Synodal Church

Let's return to where we started, with Aidan Kavanagh's famous proclamation that the liturgy is "the church caught in the act of being most overtly itself."[40] Pope Francis has expressed similar sentiments in recent apostolic letters about the liturgy, in which he describes the church's current liturgical rite as the authentic expression of the church of Vatican II.[41] For both men, questions about liturgical practice are, at their core, ecclesial questions. At stake is the fundamental question of what it means to be church and how the church ought to proceed.

Appropriating the language of Vatican II, working documents from the Synod on Synodality insist that "the Eucharist is already, in itself, the 'source and summit' of the Church's synodal dynamism."[42] Yet, the testimony and witness provided by synodal reports worldwide do

39. XVI Ordinary General Assembly, "Synodal Church in Mission," 3k-n.

40. Kavanagh, *On Liturgical Theology*, 75.

41. Pope Francis, "On the Use of the Roman Liturgy Prior to the Reform of 1970," Apostolic Letter Issued "Motu Proprio" *Traditionis Custodes* (July 16, 2021) 1; and Francis's Apostolic Letter "On the Liturgical Formation of the People of God" (*Desiderio Desideravi*) 31 and 61.

42. General Secretariat of the Synod, "Enlarge the Space of Your Tent" 89. See also 11; *Instrumentum Laboris* 30; XVI Ordinary General Assembly, "Synodal Church in Mission," 1c.

little to support this bold claim. The Working Document for the Continental Stage, for example, identifies a pattern of concern from around the world that liturgical celebrations of the Eucharist are frequently concentrated on the role of the celebrant and insufficiently inclusive and participatory, especially when it comes to the access of women to ministerial roles like preaching and the diaconate. And the quality of homilies is almost unanimously reported as a problem![43] Ultimately, the document acknowledges, "The reports [from around the world] do not fail to point out the main shortcomings of the actual celebratory praxis, which obscure [the liturgy's] synodal effectiveness."[44]

Today's challenge in our eucharistic celebrations is that too many people experience the eucharistic liturgy as the ritual maintenance of clericalism, which is the antithesis of a synodal church rather than its source and summit. The eucharistic homily is a prime example of this way of proceeding inasmuch as it is reserved exclusively to the ordained minister, with canonical instructions making clear that laypeople are never permitted to preach a eucharistic homily, never to preach at the moment of the homily in the eucharistic celebration, and never to preach during the eucharistic liturgy at all. While lay preaching, including liturgical preaching, is permitted outside of the eucharistic celebration, within the liturgy that we insist constitutes the source and summit of the church's liturgical life, the right to speak frankly, publicly, and in one's own words is reserved to the clergy alone.

43. "Enlarge the Space of Your Tent" 64, 91.
44. "Enlarge the Space of Your Tent" 93.

So, where does this leave us in terms of eucharistic preaching today? We need to be clear that, at present, the authorization of lay preaching at the moment of the eucharistic homily faces significant structural barriers in the Roman Catholic rite. For most of the church's history, the *parrhesia* of the early churches has been off-limits to the nonordained. However, as several scholars in this symposium have pointed out, this prohibition has never been accepted or readily observed![45] The work of Vatican II, with its liturgical reforms and emphasis on baptism rather than orders as the foundation for the continuation of Christ's mission on earth, opened the door to lay preaching in substantial, albeit limited and often conflicting, ways. Although legitimate debate exists among canonists about how to resolve apparent contradictions in the various legislation and instructions about lay preaching, it is clear that since the early 2000s, there has been a chilling effect on lay preaching within the Eucharist, as well as on theological discussion and debate about the issue. The laws and their authoritative interpretations present substantive canonical barriers to including lay preachers as a regular part of the Sunday Eucharist. They must be reformed to pursue this particular liturgical expression of the synodal church fully.[46]

45. Rinere, "Lay Preaching: By Whose Authority?" Joseph Johnson, "Lay Preaching at Eucharistic Liturgies: The Law and Its Critiques," *Landas* 30, no. 2 (2016). Sarah Ann Fairbanks, "Displaced Persons: Lay Liturgical Preachers at the Eucharist," *Worship* 77, no. 5 (September 2003).

46. Notable within the documents for the universal synod is the repeated affirmation that structures and canons may and likely will be reformed to reflect synodal discernment and consensus. See

But these structural barriers have not stifled the Spirit. Lay Catholics have found many opportunities to preach outside of the eucharistic celebration in both liturgical and non-liturgical contexts. Laypeople are preaching in retreat centers and hospitals and detention facilities, in religious communities and houses of religious formation, in our churches, on the streets, and, increasingly, in digital spaces like Catholic Women Preach. And, of course, laypeople also continue to preach at the Eucharist. The advocacy, for example, of Discerning Deacons to observe the Feast of St. Phoebe (which is not part of the Western liturgical calendar) by inviting women to preach during the homily shows a renewed interest in this issue at the parish level, much as this volume reveals a renewed theological interest in this topic.[47] Outside of eucharistic liturgies, Liturgies of the Word and other liturgical celebrations that include lay preaching have proven to be a dynamic context for synodal hope. My ongoing study of lay preaching during the recent pandemic lockdowns is uncovering deeply compelling accounts of this synodal dynamism.

This study centers on two liturgical communities in the United States that opted to celebrate online Liturgies of the Word instead of live-streamed eucharistic liturgies every Sunday between March 2020 and June 2021. These two communities were not unique in their pandemic celebrations of the Liturgy of the Word, nor were they the first to develop these practices. But they

---

Instrumentum Laboris 43, B3.3; XVI Ordinary General Assembly, "Synodal Church in Mission," 9m, 13d.

47. Discerning Deacons website, https://discerningdeacons.org/celebrate2023.

offer two examples of spaces and communities in which these pandemic liturgies emerged creatively, contrary to their regular Sunday practice, which was eucharistic. In some ways, these online Liturgies of the Word were deeply informed by the eucharistic rite; they used the readings in the Sunday lectionary and the ritual form of the Liturgy of the Word that comprises the first part of the Sunday eucharistic liturgy. But unlike eucharistic liturgies, these liturgies centered on the voices of the laity. For fifteen months, clergy and laity were responsible for preaching and presiding at these celebrations. In both communities, most of the preachers during this time were lay, and most of these lay preachers were women.[48] While some of these preachers had a measure of formal homiletical training, many did not. Yet week after week, these preachers broke open the Sunday lectionary readings in the midst of a global pandemic, racialized violence, economic uncertainty, and political chaos, speaking frankly and boldly in their own words of the living God who saves.

Participants described the experience of lay preaching as a compelling feature of these liturgical gatherings, both for those invited to preach and those who listened to them. Although few participants named it in such explicit terms, my assessment, which is born of reviewing hours of film, artifacts, and interviews, suggests a bit of a reality check. These pandemic liturgies gave fuller expression to the synodal church than their eucharistic counterparts, particularly when it comes to preaching.

48. Of the 122 homilies offered during this time between the two communities, sixty-nine were preached by laywomen, twenty-seven by laymen, twenty-one by priests, and three collaboratively.

Online, clergy and laity shared the responsibility for the proclamation of the Word, sometimes even sharing the work of preaching within a single homily. And while this preaching spanned a range of homiletical functions—praise, thanksgiving, grief, anger, lament, and hope, to name just a few—the work of preaching itself, shared among many calls from within the people of God whose voices were raised by the Spirit and by the community, became its proclamation of the freedom of the Gospel and the radical inclusivity of a synodal church. Another participant said, "For the first time in my life, I believe that I am the church."[49]

The lifting of local restrictions on public gatherings, the availability of protective masks and vaccines, and declining infections made it possible for these liturgical communities to return to their regular practice of Sunday Eucharists in June of 2021. And for many, this return brought with it conflicting experiences. People spoke of the joy of returning to the eucharistic meal with faces that were now even more familiar after months of gathering on Zoom. But people also lamented the loss of lay voices and leadership upon their return to the Sunday Eucharist. One participant wondered whether they would ever return to their "traditional parish liturgy," while others asked whether there was a way to retain the practice of lay preaching they had come to love within the Sunday Mass. For many, their experience of

49. Gail Porter Mandell and Jane Pitz, "A Vibrant Zoom Liturgy during COVID Lockdown Leaves Lessons for Church," *Global Sisters Report,* June 26, 2002, https://www.globalsistersreport.org/news/coronavirus/blog/vibrant-zoom-liturgy-during-covid-lockdown-leaves-lessons-church.

lay preaching during these pandemic liturgies deepened their sense of disenfranchisement during Mass, where the ritually inscribed hierarchical separation between the speaking church of the clergy and the listening church of the laity was now even more apparent. The rich tapestry of preaching that they knew online was suddenly flattened and muted in the return to a eucharistic liturgy that centers the bodies and voices of the male ordained at both ambo and altar, while full, conscious, and active participation of the laity could be fulfilled only through supporting roles. Whether or not the Eucharist will ever become the source and summit of the church's synodal dynamism, it seems clear that this is not yet the case.

But structural shifts have begun to pave the way for more substantive reforms. Pope Francis has allowed women to be formally installed as lectors, acolytes, and catechists for the first time, reviving a significant interest and conversation about lay installation into permanent liturgical ministries—a practice permitted but largely ignored for the last forty years. In his homily at the first installation of these ministers, Francis emphasized that the sixteen lectors and catechists "are called to the important work of serving the Gospel of Jesus, of proclaiming him, so that his consolation, his joy and his liberation can reach everyone." But, the pope told the assembly, "That is also the mission of each one of us: to be credible messengers, prophets of God's word in the world."[50] The explicit diversification of ministries of proclamation among the people of God, as well as a clear path for the authorization and commissioning of laypeople, especially women, into a variety of permanent

50. Francis, "Gift of the Holy Spirit," homily, January 23, 2022.

liturgical ministries is a substantive step toward a more synodal church and suggests yet another structural possibility for the inclusion of lay preaching in all areas of the church's life. The recent synod included among their proposals the expansion of the ministry of lector to include preaching.[51]

Returning to our original question: "Can a theological case be made for the church to charge or commission a more extensive and diverse pool of qualified lay preachers and evangelists to preach the Word of God at the Eucharist?" Yes, I believe the church *can* and *should* permit and commission lay preachers to preach at the Eucharist at the moment of the homily. It seems clear to me that in their current form, our eucharistic liturgies often fail to give expression to a synodal church and instead reinforce a clericalist ecclesiology that ritualizes and consecrates the voice of the clergy and the silence of the laity. If the Eucharist is to truly become "the source and summit of the church's synodal dynamism," the work of proclamation in bold speech and earnest listening are responsibilities that all of the people of God must share. Incorporating lay preaching into all of the church's liturgical celebrations, including and perhaps even the eucharistic liturgy, is essential. In the words of the October 2023 synod's synthesis report, "If the Eucharist shapes synodality, then the first step we should take is to celebrate the Mass in a way that befits the gift."[52]

51. XVI Ordinary General Assembly, "Synodal Church in Mission," 8n.

52. XVI Ordinary General Assembly, "Synodal Church in Mission," 3k.

A Word Emerging from the Whole Body of the Faithful

Martin Madar

While Dr. Layla A. Karst has approached the central question of this symposium as a liturgist, at the very start of her paper, she reminded us that "the liturgical is always also ecclesial," and I would add that "the liturgical is always ecclesiological." Dr. Karst's remarks complement the key claims of Dr. Edward Hahnenberg and move the discussion of the central question of this symposium forward not so much in a linear fashion as by examining the other side of the same coin.

Karst articulated her overarching question from the perspective of synodality, asking, "What should eucharistic preaching look like in a synodal church?" She addressed this question by reflecting on the nature and form of eucharistic preaching in the Roman Rite and in Pope Francis's emerging theology of synodality.

She has given a helpful overview of the shift that has taken place in the understanding of the liturgy from the Second Vatican Council to the present. She explained that the requirement of a homily stipulated in the instructions of the 1969 Roman Missal was an innovation compared to the standards of the previous four hundred years.

From the perspective of liturgical theology, she took issue with the reasoning that only the ordained can give a homily because the homily is liturgical in its character. She rightly pointed out that this line of reasoning makes good sense in a preconciliar liturgical theology, which reserved all liturgical actions to the clergy, who performed them on behalf of the faithful. In the postconciliar liturgical landscape, however, where all the faithful are invited to full participation in the liturgical activity, even though in distinct and ordered ways, the liturgical character of the homily does not serve as a sufficient justification for a constitutive restriction of the homily to the ordained. Karst also took issue with the claim that the homily is a priestly liturgical action. She argued that it is an action of the entire assembly, in which case the homily's liturgical minister need not be ordained.

Yves Congar made a compelling case that according to the teaching of Vatican II, the church as a whole is the subject of liturgical acts.[1] While some actions at the Eucharist are proper only to the ordained presider, others are not. Understanding the homily as an action of the entire assembly, as Karst does, justifies lay eucharistic preaching.

In addition to making a case for lay homiletic preaching from the perspective of liturgical theology, Karst presented the current promotion of synodality as a kind of *kairos* for making a constructive case for lay eucharistic preaching.

1. Yves Congar, "The *Ecclesia* or Christian Community as a Whole Celebrates the Liturgy," in *At the Heart of Christian Worship: Liturgical Essays of Yves Congar*, trans. and ed. Paul Philibert (Collegeville, MN: Liturgical Press, 2010), 15–68.

Karst noted that too many experience the eucharistic liturgy as the ritual maintenance of clericalism, which is the antithesis of a synodal church. She indicated that the eucharistic homily is a prime example of this way of proceeding inasmuch as it is reserved exclusively for the ordained preacher. In the current form, our eucharistic liturgies often fail to give expression to a synodal church and instead reinforce a clericalist ecclesiology that ritualizes and consecrates the voice of the clergy and the silence of the laity.

One idea that might make Dr. Karst's case for lay homiletic preaching even stronger has to do with the Second Vatican Council's understanding of revelation. In the council's treatment of revelation, God addresses a Word to the whole Church. The council distanced itself from a neoscholastic theology of revelation in which God communicates revelation first to the magisterium, which then transmits it to the rest of the church. The council taught instead that "the Word of God emerges within the whole body of the faithful through a complex set of ecclesial relationships in which all the baptized, professional theologians, and the college of bishops play vital and necessary roles."[2]

This teaching is crucial for the theology of synodality and for making a theological case for lay eucharistic preaching. Synodality means that the preservation and active realization of revelation are the tasks of everyone in the church.[3] Therefore, everyone in the church should

2. Richard R. Gaillardetz, *By What Authority? Foundations for Understanding Authority in the Church*, rev. and exp. ed. (Collegeville, MN: Liturgical Press, 2018), 25–26.

3. Ormond Rush, "*Dei Verbum* and the Roots of Synodality," *Theological Studies* 84, no. 4 (2023): 570–91, at 585.

be listened to. The church should exist so that no one's voice is excluded by design. Everyone's voice is vital to the reception and preservation of God's word.

Furthermore, in light of the council's teaching that the whole body of the faithful receives divine revelation, reserving the homily to a priest or deacon hinders that reception from actualizing its full potential. While in theory, the whole church is the recipient of God's word, in actual practice, when it comes to the privileged moment of hearing God's word and reflecting on it in the homily, the voices and perspectives of those not ordained are not considered.

The biggest obstacle standing in the way of lay eucharistic preaching of a homily seems more sociological than theological. From 1973 until 1981, laypersons in Germany were allowed to preach a homily with Vatican approval. Unless we consider this permission to have been granted erroneously, we can infer that priestly ordination was not regarded as intrinsic to homiletic preaching. We can infer the same from the current practice of deacons being ordinary ministers of the homily.

It is no coincidence that permission for lay homiletic preaching in Germany was withdrawn at the time when the revival of the medieval theology of the priesthood understood within a cultic or sacerdotal framework was promoted by the Vatican. A key reason for the withdrawal was attracting vocations to the priesthood. Extending various ministries to the laity was seen as obscuring the essential distinction between the ministerial priesthood and the universal priesthood of all believers. In other words, the gradual disappearance of the specialness by which seminarians or priests saw themselves vis-à-vis the laity had detrimental effects on attracting men to consider the vocation to the priesthood in terms of making sense of the costs and benefits involved. This line of thinking is at the heart of clericalism. For many, lay homiletic preaching continues to function sociologically as an obstacle to attracting vocations to the priesthood.

Nonetheless, more than a few among the ordained would welcome some relief from preaching the homily at every Mass. Preaching is a demanding task in several respects. It requires offering meaningful and inspiring reflections on Scripture week in and week out. More than a few among the ordained would welcome competent, properly instituted laywomen and men as coworkers in the homiletic vineyard. I hope that one day this possibility becomes a reality since there are no compelling theological reasons against it.

Lay Preaching in a Time of Liminality

Maurice J. Nutt

Dr. Layla A. Karst's presentation on eucharistic preaching in a synodal church conjures up a fond memory of my teacher, mentor, and servant of God, Sister Thea Bowman, FSPA, PhD's response to CBS veteran correspondent Mike Wallace about the impact of her preaching. She forthrightly responded to his question with playful sarcasm, "Oh no, I don't preach! I witness. I testify. I share the Good News of the Lord Jesus Christ. The priests can preach. You know women don't preach in the Catholic Church."[1]

Her words acknowledge her liturgical limitation. This vowed religious woman's preaching greatly inspired and influenced many Catholics in America, yet her preaching at Mass was prohibited. She best conveyed her lay preaching phenomenon in the Black Catholic community when she said, "The Word of God became incarnate. We are called to preach that word day by day by day—in

1. Sister Thea Bowman, excerpt from an interview with Mike Wallace, *60 Minutes*, CBS News, New York, May 3, 1987, https://youtu.be/SBrNlQ6fJkM?si=_hQUPVwy8ZHUghUR.

our homes, in our families, in our neighborhood—to bear witness, to testify, to shout it from the rooftops, [and] with our lives."[2]

Bowman's response to Wallace during her *60 Minutes* interview would seem humorous were it not for the restrictions on laywomen and men's preaching of the homily at eucharistic liturgies—demeaning and egregious, causing unnecessary pain, negating the import and dignity of sacramental Christian baptism, and worst of all, causing some to leave the Roman Catholic Church. As Dr. Karst lays out the restrictions for laypeople preaching at eucharistic liturgies mandated by the Code of Canon Law, she also valiantly refutes and argues how irrational these restrictions are and urges us to reimagine a synodal way forward in our discussion and discernment of lay preaching.

The presenter's task was to answer an intriguing question: "Can a theological case be made for the church to charge or commission a more extensive and diverse pool of qualified lay preachers and evangelists to preach the Word of God at the Eucharist?" The nature of the question is not threatening or provocative. It is a query regarding a possibility, inviting an idea, welcoming different perspectives, and seeking to expand what is deemed normative to engendering prophetic imagination. Yet, according to canon law, preaching at the Eucharist is exclusively the cleric's right. Canon 767 states, "Among the forms of preaching, the homily, which is part of the liturgy itself and is reserved to a priest or deacon, is

2. An excerpt from Sister Thea Bowman's "Women's Day" undated speech at Saint Clement Pope Church is from her handwritten notes for that speech, Franciscan Sisters of Perpetual Adoration archives, La Crosse, WI.

preeminent; in the homily the mysteries of faith and the norms of Christian life are to be explained from the sacred text during the course of the liturgical year."

Dr. Karst makes poignant observations and assertions regarding Pope Francis's promulgation of an emerging theology of synodality, and she issues a clarion call to become a synodal church that listens, learns, and journeys in solidarity with one another. Indeed, a church that listens before she speaks. Suppose we are to genuinely become a listening, learning, loving church that lives the mission of Jesus Christ. In that case, we must understand that this arduous but possible task will be in contention with the church's authoritative, hierarchical, clerical-centered position. There is a pervasive spirit of clericalism present among many young priests and seminarians that promotes an unhealthy and unholy sense of superiority of clerics over the laity. I agree with Rafael Luciani's quote in Karst's paper, "that this clericalist institutional model constitutes the fundamental ecclesial failure of our time."[3] On several occasions, Francis has admonished clericalism in the church. On one occasion during the October 2023 synod meeting in Rome, he described the faithful people of God as "patiently and humbly enduring the scorn, mistreatment, and marginalization of institutionalized clericalism."[4]

3. Rafael Luciani, *Synodality: A New Way of Proceeding in the Church*, trans. Joseph Owens, SJ (New York: Paulist Press, 2022), 2.

4. Courtney Maris, "Pope Francis Speaks at Synod on Synodality: 'Clericalism' Defiles the Church," Catholic News Agency, October 26, 2023, https://www.catholicnewsagency.com/news/255817/pope-francis-speaks-at-synod-on-synodality-clericalism-defiles-the-church.

I appreciate Karst's clarification that Francis's vision of a synodal church does not eliminate the distinction between ordained and lay members. Still, in Karst's words, it also does not "define that distinction by who gets to speak and who gets to listen. In a synodal church, all the baptized are understood and called to be both teachers and disciples." By the sacramental and sanctifying grace received through the waters and anointing of baptism, as duly initiated disciples and members of the Body of Christ, Catholic Christians and other baptized Christians should see it as their calling to proclaim the Good News to all they encounter. Baptism enables Christians to witness to Jesus and the kingdom of God. To witness means to announce, proclaim, testify, make known, and preach. Patricia A. Parachini, in her book titled *Lay Preaching: State of the Question*, states, "Proclaiming the gospel (preaching) is effected in many ways throughout our lives as Christian believers, especially in words and works of reconciliation, healing, and justice. We preach through the witness of our life, through teaching, through ordinary conversation and personal testimony to God's love, as well as through a more formal proclamation in worship. Preaching is the call of all the baptized."[5] There is minimal focus on the responsibility of every baptized Christian to preach the Good News, regardless of whether there is a shortage of priests and deacons. These discussions imply the unspoken assumption that if there were enough clergy to preach, laypersons would not need to preach at eucharistic liturgies.

5. Patricia A. Parachini, *Lay Preaching: State of the Question*, American Essays in Liturgy (Collegeville, MN: Liturgical Press, 1999), 5.

This presumption totally negates the call or vocation of the laity to preach. Again, this perspective is mired in clericalism. Karst calls it "the ritual maintenance of clericalism, which is the antithesis of a synodal church rather than its source and summit."

There is also little acknowledgment of the value of lay preaching in enhancing the expression of the preached Word. Liturgical preaching is almost always monolithic, meaning that the only voice and faith perspective heard among congregations is from a male, clerical, celibate, dominant cultural position. Thus, Roman Catholic liturgical preaching remains oppressively limited because important other and necessary voices are silenced and hindered. Ironically, the Catholic community gathers to celebrate liturgy with "full, conscious, and active participation" as the Body of Christ—to be and to fully experience the Body of Christ communally among themselves and in the sacrament, yet representation at the table of the Word and the table of the Eucharist is restricted and does not signify this profound reality.

Dr. Karst argues that, historically, liturgical practices have "functioned as a sort of enacted *sensus fidei*, affirming and even giving rise to theologies that are eventually accepted as doctrines and practices that eventually become normative. But liturgical practices have also been responsive to changing and evolving theological expressions, understandings, and commitments." I found most insightful her position that liturgical reform happens when the church's liturgical practice is inconsistent with its current ecclesiology. Additionally, conflicts and discussions about liturgy are frequently carried out in support of conflicting ecclesiologies, as evidenced in various areas of our Church today. I think conflicting ecclesiologies regarding liturgical practices will remain if there is an unwillingness to read "the signs of the times" and a rejection of synodal accompaniment.

Finally, in responding to Dr. Karst's discerning and percipient paper, I have framed my observations through the anthropological and sociological construct of liminality. Liminality is a concept that refers to the transitional stage or period between two different phases or states, where groups experience ambiguity, disorientation, and a sense of being "betwixt and between." I hold that the question of lay preaching within eucharistic liturgies finds the church precisely in a moment of liminality. It begs the question, "Should what is, always be?" Although the church is slow to evolve, the reality and the "signs of the times" indicate that in certain spaces of the Roman Catholic Church lay preaching happens regularly. At times, local bishops, following the complementary norm, permit the lay faithful to provisionally preach "in certain circumstances or when it seems useful in particular cases"[6] or because a particular faith community deems that lay preaching is essential to their spiritual and liturgical enrichment. At times, the local ordinary condemns this lay preaching, and the community must navigate less satisfying practices such as laypeople giving a "reflection" after a priest or deacon gives the sanctioned "official homily." As the church continues in this liminal phase of challenging existing norms and exploring new possibilities of lay preaching, I firmly believe that lay preaching in eucharistic liturgies will become acceptable

6. "USCCB Decree Implementing Canon 766 of the Code of Canon Law," USCCB Committee on the Liturgy Newsletter XXXVII (December 13, 2001): 49–50.

and that the ambo will be a shared space between the ordained and laity. Then, along with the lay participant that Dr. Karst told us about who preached during the pandemic and who said, "For the first time in my life, I believe that I am the church," a genuinely grateful and inclusive synodal church will be able, with enthusiasm, to say, "Amen!"

Participant Essays

New Testament Basis for Preaching

Barbara E. Reid

I am a Dominican sister, a member of the Order of Preachers. I have been taught by Dominican sisters my entire life, beginning in the first grade. As a youngster, I wanted to be a teacher like them. We never talked about preaching in those days—that was a term that Protestants used. After I joined my Dominican community, when people asked me what the OP stood for after my name, I would translate: "Order of Preachers," but quickly add that we women exercise the preaching charism by teaching.

When the Second Vatican Council directed that we return to the charism of our founder, we women Dominicans began to reclaim our charism of preaching. But there was one huge obstacle to our being able to embrace that gift fully: in our church, the authority to preach at Eucharist—the venue where most Catholic preaching occurs—is linked with ordination, to which women are not admitted. Some of us make peace with this anomaly by asserting that we preach always in everything we do and say. While that certainly is true, that stance does not resolve the underlying difficulty. Others of us have deliberately pursued the study of Scripture and theology and have learned public speaking skills that would prepare us to use our gift for preaching in professional ministries. We seek every opportunity to preach at prayer services, Morning and Evening Prayer, communion services, wakes, etc. In collaboration with our brother priests, some of us push the envelope a little further, preaching in our motherhouse communities at Eucharist, especially on occasions such as funerals, jubilees, and professions of our sisters. In 1973, the *Directory for Masses with Children* allowed, "With the consent of the pastor or rector of the church, nothing forbids one of the adults who is participating in a Mass with children from speaking to the children after the gospel reading, especially if the priest finds it difficult to adapt himself to the mentality of children."[1] We reasoned that women religious, as well as other laywomen and men, deserve the same consideration as children—that the preacher be one who can speak our language. Some dance around the prohibition of lay preaching at Eucharist by calling the preaching by laypersons a "reflection" rather than a "homily." In some instances, to keep the letter of the law, the lay "reflection" will be preceded by a one- or two-sentence "homily" by the priest.

It is becoming increasingly evident that the whole Church is poorer from hearing the Word broken open week after week, year after year, only from the perspectives of ordained men. When a woman preaches, something different happens within those who hear. Women

1. Congregation for Divine Worship, *Directory for Masses with Children* (Washington, DC: United States Catholic Conference, 1974) 24.

preachers often see things in the text and its implications for our lives of faith that are not as apparent to our brothers. For example, a woman breaking open the story of the Canaanite woman who pleads with Jesus to heal her daughter is more likely to identify with the woman rather than Jesus and to liken her own experiences of being ignored and shut out by powerful men to that of the mother in the text. She may be better able to help females in the congregation relate their experiences to the Canaanite woman's persistence, often a woman's most powerful tool in the face of adversity. She may also be able to help the men in the congregation understand an aspect of women's experience they might not have previously recognized and move them toward becoming allies in the struggle.

Women preachers often ask different questions about the text; for example: Where were the women and children? In the story of the feeding of the five thousand, for instance, Mark ends with "Those who had eaten the loaves numbered five thousand men" (6:44). In contrast, Matthew concludes the story, "And those who ate were about five thousand men, besides women and children" (14:21). When women and children are not mentioned in the text, women preachers will more often than not reflect on their overlooked presence and experiences. Women preachers are inclined to explore the effect the text has on contemporary women who hear it. They may wonder about the reaction of the women who prayed and prophesied in the Corinthian assembly or that of the deacon Phoebe in Cenchreae when they heard Paul's letter to them read aloud, where he admonished, "[W]omen should be silent in the churches. For they are not permitted to speak, but should be subordinate, as the law also says" (1 Cor 14:34). Would they have pushed back or simply assented to Paul's instructions? How should contemporary women respond to such a directive?

As the church confronts the question of the admissibility of lay preachers to break open the Word at Eucharist, one key consideration is the biblical foundation for such. There is no question that the ministry of the Word was central to both Jesus' mission and that of his earliest followers. The first thing that Jesus does at the outset of his mission is to preach (*kēryssein*) good news (Mark 1:14). When Paul lists the gifts given the community, he gives first place to apostles, prophets, and teachers—that is, those who exercise ministries of the Word (1 Cor 12:28). In Acts of the Apostles, the Twelve refuse to cede ministry of the Word (*diakonia tou logou*) to the newly appointed Hellenist ministers who will focus on service of the table (*diakonia trapezais*) (Acts 6:2, 4).

In the gospels and the letters of Paul, we see both women and men followers of Jesus depicted as proclaiming the Good News. In the early church, of course, there was no lay-ordained distinction among those who ministered. Those whom Jesus formed for a preaching ministry include not only the Twelve (Matt 10:5-16 // Mark 6:7-13 // Luke 9:1-6) but also Galilean women. In what follows, I will focus on the women who preach in various ways in the New Testament.

In the middle of the Galilean ministry, Luke describes Jesus going "through cities and villages, proclaiming [*kēryssōn*] and bringing the good news." With him were the Twelve, as well as Mary Magdalene, Joanna, Susanna, and many others (Luke 8:1-3). At the end of the gospel, Mary Magdalene, Joanna, Mary the mother of James, and the other women with them announce (*apēngeilan*) the good news to the eleven and the rest (Luke 24:9; similarly, Matt 28:8-10; John 20:18). In the Gospel of John, many townspeople in Samaria come to believe in Jesus "because of the woman's testimony" who had encountered him at the well (John 4:39).

Several women in the New Testament exercise the gift of prophecy, which is one form of preaching. The prophet Anna spent eighty-four years in the temple, worshipping, fasting, and praying until she saw the long-awaited Savior. She then spoke "about the child to all who were looking for the redemption of Jerusalem" (Luke 2:38). While they are not explicitly called prophets, Jesus' mother and Elizabeth make prophetic proclamations in Luke's first chapter. Elizabeth makes an important theological declaration when she says that God delights in removing humiliation from suffering people, herself included (1:25). Likewise when she pronounces Mary blessed and her child "my Lord," she articulates a profound understanding of incarnation (Luke 1:39-45). Mary's *Magnificat* is a prophetic utterance that gives voice to God's dream for human flourishing, where none go hungry and those crushed by humiliation and oppression are raised up (1:46-55). In his second volume, while Luke does not disclose their names or the content of their proclamations, he says that Philip the evangelist had four virgin daughters with the gift of prophecy (Acts 21:9). In the Corinthian community, some women pray and prophesy in the assembly (1 Cor 11:5).

The Corinthian community also boasts of Phoebe, deacon (*diakonos*) and leader (*prostatis*) of the Church of Cenchreae, one of Corinth's port cities (Rom 16:1-2). The noun *diakonos* and the verb *dikonein* refer to a wide variety of ministries, including ministries of the Word (e.g., Acts 6:4). It is reasonable to imagine Phoebe exercising ministries of preaching, teaching, and evangelizing as she leads her community. Another woman Paul greets at the end of his letter to the Romans is Junia, whom he says is "prominent among the apostles" (Rom 16:7). Apostolic ministry is customarily associated with preaching the Gospel.

Another woman Paul greets in Romans 16:3-4, also featured in Acts of the Apostles, is Prisca (or Priscilla as Luke calls her). Luke recounts that in Ephesus there was an eloquent preacher named Apollos, who had come from Alexandria. When Priscilla and Aquila heard him, they noted that there were deficiencies in what he had learned, and so they "explained [*ektithēmi*] the Way of God to him more accurately" (Acts 18:24-26).

In the gospels and Pauline letters, ministries of the Word are central to the spread of the gospel. Women and men announce Good News, prophesy, bring others to belief in Jesus based on their word, preach, teach, and evangelize. Nonetheless, then as now, some insisted that ministries of the Word belonged solely to men. In Acts of the Apostles, Peter and Paul predominate as preachers. Some texts in Paul's letters and the deuteropauline writings attempt to restrict and silence women. In 1 Corinthians 14:34-36, as noted above, women are told to be silent in the churches, that it is shameful for a woman to speak there. In the Pastoral Letters, we find assertions such as, "Let a woman learn in silence with full submission. I permit no woman to teach or to have authority over a man; she is to keep silent" (1 Tim 2:11-12). And while older women are recognized as teachers, they may only teach younger women, not men (Titus 2:4).

As the church grapples with commissioning laypeople to preach at the Eucharist, there is strong biblical evidence that both women and men exercised this ministry in the early church. Texts such as 1 Corinthians 14:34-36, 1 Timothy 2:11-12, and Titus 2:4 need to be understood in their historical context as coming from a patriarchal worldview that stood in strong contrast to the reality of how the Spirit was bestowing gifts on believers without regard to gender and status. As the Spirit continues to endow women and men, lay and ordained, with the charism for preaching, and as laywomen and laymen develop the biblical and theological expertise and rhetorical skills to exercise this gift well, the church will flourish all the more when these gifts are fully welcomed.

God Save the People, for Thine They Are

Elissa Rinere

These few words come from a song in *Jesus Christ Superstar*, the Broadway musical that was so popular in the 1970s. As portrayed in the play, the song is a strident plea for God to take action and do something. But how does God usually save the people from war, famine, desperation, and aimlessness? God raises up prophets.

Prophets come in all shapes and sizes. Prophets see what others might not see. Prophets see a light—a solution, a means of rescuing the suffering people—and call on others to follow the path toward the light. Prophetic inspirations can be large or small, universal or local. Whichever they might be, the church, the people of God, is enriched when prophetic lights are discerned and followed.

If we look around at the situation of the church in the United States, what do we see? This country has goodness and holiness, generosity and mission. But we can also see fewer people in the pews, fewer parishes, and fewer priests to staff the parishes. There are fewer baptisms of infants, fewer Catholic marriages, and even fewer religious funeral services for Catholics who have died.

These declines in Church life have complicated roots, with layer upon layer of accretion over many years. What are we to do? Is this a time to pray, "God save the people"? Or is it time to look for some small prophetic light to lead the way to a brighter path? The symposium on lay preaching at the Eucharist that was held at Aquinas Institute of Theology in St. Louis is such a prophetic light, pointing the way to deeper enrichment and inclusion for all God's people.

Certainly, we are aware of the of the trajectory the laity have been on since Vatican II, from reception of salvation through obedience and observance, to active participation in the life and ministry of the church, thereby choosing to be disciples of Jesus, not merely receivers of the ministry of others. The notion that the priesthood of the ordained and the priesthood of the baptized must work together to bring about the realization of the church is no longer a disputed point in ecclesiology.

Our recent symposium on "The Pastoral Charge for Lay Catholic Eucharistic Preaching" has recommended a revision or restatement of canon 767 §1, which restricts the homily at the Eucharist to the priest or the deacon. As seen in an annotated edition of the 1983 Code of Canon Law, the sources listed for canon 767 §1, especially the conciliar documents, emphasize the importance of Scripture as the basis for sound teaching and preaching. Is preaching the homily, therefore, best left to the ordained?

Canon 766, a companion to canon 767 §1, allows for lay preaching in a church or oratory "if necessity requires it in certain circumstances or it seems advantageous in particular cases, according to the prescripts of the conference of bishops."[1]

With a few changes, this canon is a repeat of canon 1342 in the 1917 Code of Canon Law. The sources cited for this canon go back to the fourteenth and fifteenth centuries when preaching by laity was considered a form of heresy.

The road to lay preaching at eucharistic celebrations, which we currently pursue, has two obstacles: the preeminent role given to the homily both liturgically and as an exercise of the ministry of the Word (c. 767 §1) and the fear that has been carried forward for many centuries in church law and practice that preaching by laity runs the risk of departing from correct doctrine (c. 766).

Our proposal to revise canon 767 §1 focuses on the principles developed in the first session of the Synod on Synodality, held in Rome in October 2023. Synodality envisions the church as all the disciples of Jesus walking together in unity and peace. Synodality calls for the discernment of charism at all levels of the church. This discernment would ensure that the gifts of the Spirit are respected and employed for the benefit of the whole people of God.

Perhaps, in the mode of synodality, a renewed study of lay preaching might focus on a few other canons of the 1983 Code, specifically, canons in Book 2, titled "The People of God," under the subheading "The Christian Faithful." The Christian faithful are all the baptized, clergy and laity alike. These canons, among others, lay the

1. Canon Law Society of America, *Code of Canon Law: Latin-English Edition* (Washington, DC: Canon Law Society of America, 1983).

foundation for the formation of the community, which is the church. They are deeply embedded in the theology of the Second Vatican Council and have no other sources except documents issued from that council. Also, these canons are fundamental to understanding the ministerial character of baptism. These canons are the foundation of the evolution from a passive, receptive laity with respect to clergy to the vision of an active and ministerial laity in partnership with clergy.

Take, for instance, canon 204, which states, in part, that all the Christian faithful are "incorporated in Christ through baptism . . . to exercise the mission which God has entrusted to the Church to fulfill in the world." The primary source of this canon is the dogmatic constitution *Lumen Gentium*.

Or consider canon 208, building on the ministerial nature of baptism, which teaches that due to their rebirth in Christ, all the Christian faithful share "true equality regarding dignity and action by which they all cooperate in the building up of the Body of Christ according to each one's own condition and function." The primary sources for this canon are *Lumen Gentium* and *Gaudium et Spes*, with the latter of the two documents emphasizing the vital connection between the holiness of marriage and family with the vitality of the whole Church. Laypeople preaching at the Eucharist could make this vital connection between the health and holiness of marriage and the health and holiness of the church.

Canon 211 directs all the Christian faithful, laity and clergy alike, to work so that the message of salvation reaches more and more people. Again, the primary source is *Lumen Gentium*, but *Ad Gentes* also speaks to the church's missionary activity. All the Christian faithful, clergy and laity, are called to evangelize. The document states: "The work of evangelization [is] the fundamental task of the people of God" (AG 35).

These three canons are fundamental to the growth of the synodal church. They are built on the foundation of baptism as a sacrament of mission and ministry. *Lumen Gentium* envisioned this essential unity of clergy and laity on behalf of God's mission in the church: "Many benefits for the church are to be expected from this familiar relationship between the laity and the pastors. The laity's sense of their own responsibility is strengthened, their zeal is encouraged, they are more ready to add their strengths to the work of their pastors. The pastors, helped by the experience of the laity, are enabled to judge more clearly and more appropriately in spiritual and in temporal matters. Strengthened by all its members, the church can thus more effectively fulfil its mission for the life of the world" (LG 37).

As we propose a revision or restatement of canon 767 §1, we hope for the new possibilities of this canon to be examined in the prophetic light of charism, theology, ministry, and synodality. We hope for the discernment, recognition, and exercise of gifts. We hope that through this new practice of lay eucharistic preaching, the church will be enriched and God will once again have acted to save the beloved people.

It Is Happening Already

A Socio-Ecclesiological Approach to Lay Eucharistic Preaching

Maxime Allard

In this contribution, I will open a new line of argument concerning a "socio-ecclesiology" of lay eucharistic preaching. This new ecclesiological approach uses tools from pragmatic French sociologists and recent authors from the Frankfurt School of Critical Theory to analyze the already circulating theologically sound arguments in favor of lay eucharistic preaching and the resistance to these arguments on the part of many. From the start, it is essential to note that tensions are not necessarily a struggle between a hierarchy and a laity. The fissure happens differently: some laypeople, parish priests, bishops, and cardinals push for this, whereas others resist. Sometimes, the fissure or tension is presented rhetorically as an abyss or a gulf, whereas the gap is more like a ford (*gué*) that could easily be crossed.

Why such a novelty with a barbaric-sounding noun ("socio-ecclesiology")? For two reasons that are intertwined. First, we propose an ecclesiological interpretation of the resistances and their modalities within the church to the current proper theological arguments for lay eucharistic preaching and work through these negative responses to suggest new modes and regimes of argumentation. Second, we propose to operate theologically with a refined interpretation of social regimes of interactions within the Church—beyond the usually unreflected social and political tools at work in an institution—proposing and manifesting at the same time a specific sacramental life form as anticipation of the kingdom of God.

I will proceed in three stages. The first one attempts to assess the current situation almost naively but already with a somewhat critical eye. The second moment will use propositions from Luc Boltanski's pragmatic sociological reflections. The last stage will bring in elements from a specific recent strand of propositions from the Frankfurt School. Throughout, attention to the emotion involved in the rhetoric of the arguments for and against lay eucharistic preaching will be the occasion of my attempt to deepen the critique of the resistance to lay eucharistic preaching. The question of lay eucharistic preaching is not, first and foremost, an academic theoretical question or just a structural one. Baptized persons are involved and intertwined differently in the diverse ecclesial cultures within the church of God. Some suffer from the situation and experience it as an aberration or dysfunction causing injustice. Some hope for change or positive alterations toward better recognition of the effects of baptism and confirmation. Others fear not being recognized or being "mutilated" as Christians. Some dare to preach, and others are more or less angered by the whole situation, seen as damaging to the faith of individuals and the life of the church itself.

All in all, this points to a desire for a more authentic integration of all in the church of God as such and as it symbolically manifests its sacramentality when celebrating the Eucharist. But, as a hypothesis, one might not be able to reach a universally acceptable situation as the church of God is a church of churches rooted in local cultures and rhythms. Yet, where the questions arise urgently, space for experimentation must be allowed.

A First Almost Naive Appreciation

Lay eucharistic preaching is happening already—here and there, in different ways, in diverse ecclesial communities assembled to celebrate the Eucharist. It is a fact; men and women preach at the moment of the homily, with different levels of preparation and permission. We do not have a scientific survey of the practice throughout the Catholic Church, but many can attest and tell stories of having done it, seen and heard it, and appreciated it. When one hears about it, three attitudes, or emotional and intellectual postures, emerge—praise, blame, or a "So what?" response. But the praise is ambiguous: praised is the courage of the person having done it, or the praise goes for the content as excellent or much better than that of the usual priest, or, finally, praised is the novelty, the change, for change's sake. The blame is also ambivalent: it may be against the content or its rendition; it can be about the person (man or woman) taking the place of the lawful homilist; or it may come from a listener's intolerance to change.

Lay preaching at the Eucharist is taking place. It has the form and content of a homily but is not recognized as such since it is proclaimed by a nonordained minister and not by a validly mandated priest. Yet, for years, arguments—theological, canonical, liturgical, historical, and others—have been circulated within academia and the church at different local and universal levels.[1] History, official church documents from councils, popes, Roman congregations, dicasteries, and bishops have been interpreted charitably, attentively, and inventively. Tones have varied. The rhetorical element has not always been the same. This circulation could often, unfortunately, be designated as a "dialogue of the deaf"[2] or flatly rejected as inadmissible and unacceptable, considering Catholic tradition. But the arguments are there, thanks to the ongoing lay eucharistic preaching.

Even those who refuse to acknowledge the theological possibility or practical reality of lay eucharistic preaching do so in a partial or contorted manner—looking at it as a gesture against the law and thus to be blamed and punished, or as something to be described and named differently and therefore as something that may be tolerated and for which authorized delimitations and permissions may be given. The first type of acknowledgment concerns the regulated procedures present in canon law. Interestingly, those taking this stance do not punish lay preachers at the Eucharist so much as denounce them with a slap on the wrist and a subtle suggestion to call

1. This book is a witness to this and to the fact that many arguments were already proposed in the eighties and nineties, that they partially disappeared from the radar for a while, and that they are resurfacing with new propositions benefiting from ongoing historical, liturgical and theological research.

2. Marc Angenot, *Dialogues de sourds. Traité de rhétorique antilogique* (Paris: Mille et une nuits [Fayard], 2008).

things differently. The second type of acknowledgment is more interesting, as it reconfigures the practice without changing the fundamental rules. The church could institute a new ministry of lay eucharistic preacher, or ancient ministries could be reconfigured to allow eucharistic preaching for men and women alike. For example, one could consider reinstating deaconesses or, in the wake of the recent Synod on Synodality, think of rejuvenating the ministry of lector, which has received a new twist since Pope Francis opened it to women recently.

This second type of acknowledgment can be seen as a strategy developed by those who are, in fact, for the status quo and who expect that the laity will accept to remain within the parameters structuring the current state of affairs. This strategy gives hope to some while not creating too much frustration or fury among others. Yet this hope has a dark side. One will keep desiring and pushing forward through the openings proposed and offered. It is one of domination, in which one subjects oneself willingly. This phenomenon of obedience, known in political philosophy as voluntary servitude, has been understood since La Boétie's seminal text in the sixteenth century.[3] More recently, Axel Honneth shows how some types of recognition can be disguised ways to foster submission. He gives the examples of Uncle Tom, the long-standing celebration of the housewife and her virtues, and media portrayals of women that support a sexual division of labor.[4] Indeed, in the church, beyond

3. Etienne de La Boétie, *Discourse on Voluntary Servitude* (CreateSpace, 2018).

4. Axel Honneth, "La reconnaissance comme idéologie," in *La société du mépris* (Paris: La découverte, 2006), 245–74. One could

the sound theological arguments for the recognition of the laity, there are rhetorics of recognition at work that generate hope or act as "opium" so that not much changes at the legislative or pastoral levels in terms of actually effective recognition, giving rise to transformative practice, lay eucharistic preaching being possibly one of these.

However, one could also choose to see lay eucharistic preaching otherwise. One would then have to use new conceptual tools to analyze the resistance to reality and the possible acceptance of playing within a delimited field of recognized possibilities for identified agents. I propose an approach in two moments. Both will be attentive to the rhetorical elements of the arguments and spaces of discussion.

Some Pragmatic Considerations

The first moment is informed by Luc Boltanski and Laurent Thévenot's propositions in their celebrated book *On Justification: Economies of Worth* and Boltanski's collaboration with Eve Ciapello in *The New Spirit of Capitalism*.[5] These authors have developed an approach to

---

also think of Stanley Cavell's work on some categories of films in *Pursuits of Happiness: The Hollywood Comedy of Remarriage* (Cambridge: Harvard University Press, 1984) and *Contesting Tears: The Hollywood Melodrama of the Unknown Woman* (Chicago: University of Chicago Press, 1996).

5. Luc Boltanski and Laurent Thévenot, *On Justification: Economies of Worth* (Princeton: Princeton University Press, 2006); Luc Boltanski and Eve Ciapello, *The New Spirit of Capitalism* (London: Verso Books, repr. 2018). Cf. also Simon Susen and Bryan S. Turner, eds., *The Spirit of Luc Boltanski: Essays on the 'Pragmatic Sociology of Critique'* (London: Anthem Press, 2014).

types of societies that differentiate them into cities, each generating its "world." Without going too deeply into their discussion and classification, I propose that the events of lay preaching of a homily during the Eucharist and the arguments in favor of this preaching stem from a specific type of city or world and that the ignorance or rejection of these arguments and events stem from another city or world even within the same church of God. This mode of interaction between two cities is called "compromise," the promise of a capacity to understand the viewpoint of the other to the point of cooperating and coordinating efforts. Furthering his reflection in discussion with the Frankfurt School, on the invitation of Axel Honneth, Boltanski exposed three tests or trials (*épreuves*) that can happen in any city or world. These are the test of truth, the test of reality, and the test of existentialism.[6] What is happening in the church around the question of lay eucharistic preaching is a divergence of interpretation of the different tests (truth tests, reality tests, existential tests). These tests are "instances of confirmation endowed with a semantic function."[7] Employed by institutions, they reveal what performances are acceptable and the changes or transformations required to augment and strengthen the positive responses to the institutions' structures.

The *truth test*[8] is the simplest. It rests on the adequation of an action or judgment to the rules of what is acceptable.

6. Luc Boltanski, *On Critique: A Sociology of Emancipation* (Cambridge, UK: Polity, 2011), 103.

7. Boltanski, *On Critique*, 103.

8. Boltanski, 103–4 : "They strive to deploy in stylized fashion, with a view to consistency and saturation, a certain pre-established

In this sense, the current situation concerning lay eucharistic preaching is an inadequation of those who practice or argue for it according to the rules of acceptability. It requires control of the situation so that what is unacceptable either does not happen or gets redressed.

The *test of reality*[9] is different and concerns a deeper appreciation. It is not so much about the adequation of practices to already accepted performance structures. It happens when these accepted structures are questioned to conform to what is happening in line with the shared objectives. In the case of lay eucharistic preaching, the current rules are inadequate to achieve a *koinonia* of baptized sharing in the three *muneras* of Christ. This test may lead to adaptation or transformations of the rule, as seen with the changes proposed to the ministry of lector.

state of the relationship between symbolic forms and states of affairs, in such a way as to constantly reconfirm it. The state of affairs whose reality and value are to be confirmed is established in token situations which, to the maximum extent, possess the properties of the type situations that correspond to them, with which they are supposed to coincide."

9. Boltanski, 105–6: They "are employed to face up to critique in a situation of dispute, always liable to lead to violence. They have the character of tests. They make it possible to put to the test the reality of the claims of beings, especially human beings, by confronting them with their ability to satisfy the corresponding requirements, stabilized by qualifications and formats. To adopt the Aristotelian distinction, we can say that the *powers* of these beings must then be revealed by *acts* performed in specific conditions and in contact with systems of objects. In other cases, it is the test itself that is put to the test, and one then examines whether the way in which it is conducted here and now, in some particular situation, fully conforms to the form and pre-established procedures that should govern its course."

The last type of test, the *existential test*,[10] is the aspect of the situation concerning lay eucharistic preaching that is probably least appreciated for what it is by the groups and instances resisting it. They often remain at the level of the existing rules or the possible flexibility of those or new ones, not paying attention to the emotional impact of the current situation, nor the rhetoric of complaint accompanying it and how negative emotions serve as a tool for generalization and socio-ecclesiological critique. At this level, the argumentation needs to be refined and adjusted if liberating and fair transformations are to happen.

Toward a Critique of an Ecclesial Form of Life

Another way of seeing this is to say that the first two types of tests stand within a form of life, whereas the

10. Boltanski, 107: "Unlike the first two, existential tests must not be regarded as having been subject to a process of institutionalization, so that they retain an individual—or, as people say, 'lived'—character even when they affect a large number of people, but each of them taken in isolation. Only their sharing can confer a 'collective' character on them. The latter is liable in its turn to be foregrounded to support demands, criticize existing reality tests and, if necessary, demand that new ones be introduced—and this in order to sanction *acknowledgement* of offensive factors that have hitherto remained unacknowledged, in the sense that they could be *seen* but without being *identified* or integrated into the domain of reality. In the case of existential tests, another of the meanings that can be taken by the word test prevails over the one predominant in the case of the reality test. It refers to what provokes suffering, at least psychic, what *affects*. Existential tests are based on experiences, like those of injustice or humiliation, sometimes with the shame that accompanies them, but also, in other cases, the joy created by transgression when it affords access to some form of authenticity."

third one, because of its focus on the work and effect of the negative in the form of life, calls for an overall critique of this form of life. With this idea of a possible, appropriate, and opportune critique of the current ecclesial form of life, I wish to engage in this second moment of analysis of the experiences of lay eucharistic preaching and the tensions surrounding it.

The question and events surrounding lay eucharistic preaching are not ecclesial, liturgical, or canonical problems that must be solved. It is also not a growth crisis—a category *Gaudium et Spes* used to talk about disconcerting events and tensions from the perspective of a naturally developing organism.[11] It is a symptom of a life in need of critical assessment. For this section, I will find my inspiration in Rahel Jaeggi's *Critique of Form of Life* and Marc Maesschalck's presentation of it.[12]

The current situation of lay eucharistic preaching is one of dissatisfaction, fundamentally expressing a desire for a more authentic ecclesial form of life. These dissatisfactions and the intertwined hopes give rise to a renewed sensitivity to modes of expression of faith that the felt unidimensionality of theological, institutional, and canonical forms of ecclesial life have marginalized. One of the new sensitivities is for expressing one's faith in eucharistic preaching by men and women competent to do so. These dissatisfactions foster the production of theological discourses supporting the baptized who are

11. *Gaudium et Spes* 4: "A transformation of this kind brings with it the serious problems associated with any crisis of growth."

12. Rahel Jaeggi, *Critique of Form of Life* (Cambridge: Harvard University Press, 2018); Marc Maesschalck, "L'urgence d'une critique des formes de vie," *Revue Théologique de Louvain* 54 (2023): 210–40.

motivated and feel called and moved by the Spirit to preach. But the consciousness of this is not sufficient. Questions arise: How may the conditions and modalities of a new or renewed form of ecclesial life be conceived and thought of as operational in the ecclesial space? How may one imagine and think of a genetic totality—the church—that engenders from within itself a multiplicity of accepted behaviors and actions participating in the common impulse and instinct from the Spirit to be the sacrament of the kingdom to come? How may this be done when the ideal norm is not present at hand or the property of any group within the church but will only be manifested eschatologically and when the regulation of this ideal normative principle is present as a complex of biblical and ecclesial metaphors, practices, and discourses throughout its history and called tradition? How can this be done? This tradition is the object of constant conflicts of interpretation since interpretation is an ongoing process inscribed in a specific form of institution. How can a critique help move from passivity to a critical stance that does not let itself be transformed into a new form of submission? How can this critique become empowering? These questions cannot be answered here.

I will propose a particular aspect of a critique of the ecclesial form of life within which the question of lay eucharistic preaching arises. I hypothesize that a fundamental unthematized inherited condition that engenders the current multiplicity of behaviors—with some attempting to restrict any change or belief in change and others being marginalized or made invisible—is rooted in the idea and experience of sacrality.

Early on in the experience of being the church of God in the world, liturgy was integrated into the field of the sacred. Then, the church itself was consecrated.[13] Slowly but irrepressibly, the clergy officiating sacred acts in a sacred building became sacrosanct.[14] This "sacralization" is still present in the documents of the Second Vatican Council.[15] This process of sacralization contributed to separating the place, the action, and the persons participating in the Eucharist from the rest of the human

13. Dominique Iogna-Prat, *La Maison Dieu. Une histoire monumentale de l'Église au Moyen Âge* (Paris: Éditions du Seuil, 2006).

14. Joseph Famérée, "Le ministère ordonné selon Vatican II: avancées et limites," *Revue théologique de Louvain* 53, no. 4 (2022): 409–35; Philippe Martin, "Christianisation? Déchristianisation? Rechristianisation? La question de la sacralisation de l'espace dans la France catholique (XIXe–XXe siècles)," *Kirchliche Zeitgeschichte* (1998): 51–68; Henri de Montety, "Les carrières ecclésiastiques: professionnalisation et sacralization," *Revue des Deux Mondes* (2013): 90–94; Serge Gruzinski, "Christianisation ou occidentalisation? Les sources romaines d'une anthropologie historique," *Mélanges de l'école française de Rome* 101, no. 2 (1989): 733–50; Jean-François Chiron, "Le 'sacerdoce' dans le discours catholique avant Vatican II," *Recherches de science religieuse* 109, no. 2 (2021): 239–65.

15. There is no study, that I know of, analyzing the use of "sacr-" in Vatican II documents and the dialectic it entertains with "sanct-." But here are a few—in no way a complete survey—of the instances where it is used: the liturgy is sacra (*Sacrosanctum Concilium* 1, 9, 11, 12, 14, 15, 16; *Presbyterium Ordinis* 5; *Optatam Totius* 1, 16) and its actions are also (*Sacrosanctum Concilium* 18 and *Presbyterium Ordinis* 12) as are rites (*Sacrosanctum Concilium* 7; *Lumen Gentium* 7); Scripture is (*Sacrosanctum Concilium* 7; *Lumen Gentium* 14; *Optatam Totius* 16); ministry is (*Lumen Gentium* 13; *Presbyterium Ordinis* 17 and 19; *Optatam Totius* 19); ordination is (*Presbyterium Ordinis* 1, 2, 7; *Optatam Totius* 8); pastors are (*Sacrosanctum Concilium* 11); science/theology is (*Presbyterium Ordinis* 19); celibacy for the priests is (*Presbyterium Ordinis* 16) along with the discipline pertaining to their life (*Presbyterium Ordinis* 19). This quick survey is sufficient to see the presence of the sacred moving from one field to the other.

experience. It also, for the question of lay eucharistic preaching, separates the baptized one from another.[16]

What is clear, though, is that one needs not maintain in the life of the church the forms of sacrality rooted in the Old Testament's mythical experiences of the sacred, nor those of the Greco-Roman religions from which the early churches borrowed, nor from the Merovingian forms at work in the High Middle Ages, nor from those post-Reformation forms fighting the Protestant deflation of rituals and the emergence of a modern form of the sacrality of the monarch, nor the Romantic nineteenth-century nostalgic one that inspired the liturgical renewals of that era, nor, finally, the ones dreamt of or fantasized by certain neoconservative groups in the Catholic Church currently. There are no comprehensive historical and theological assessments of the transformations, displacements, and novelties concerning the sacred and sacrality in the experience of being the church of God in history, nor of how it is used argumentatively in different theological productions throughout this complex experience.[17] Thus, if one thinks liturgy, church, and

16. "Separations" come in many forms and types, and their acceptability change over time. The history of theological discussions on laity since Yves Congar's seminal works are all about thinking distinction so as to unite—to mimic a title from Jacques Maritain—and not anymore about separating by sacralization related to the notions of impurity (ritual and others that were taboo) in a modern context. Not that these do not exist and have no effect on human interactions or socialization processes, but they are not accepted any more as regulatory norms—and this is partly due to the preaching of the Gospel and a certain christianization of European populations over centuries.

17. The best introduction to this question may be found in Jean-Claude Schmitt, "La notion de sacré et son application à l'histoire

priests need to be sacred, one must reflect on the stakes linked to this category and why it was introduced, reiterated, and inflated. Only such a theological labor with close attention to historical, anthropological, and socio-ecclesiological aspects would prepare for this. Furthermore, this would need to be done in dialogue with the new forms of sacredness emerging in the world.

Conclusion: Opening Experimental Transitional Spaces

But as we wait for this, as this will take "a little while" (John 16:16-17), one may choose to offer space and time for experimentations, which would not be mere concessions nor simply tolerated. One needs more than fragmented, intermittent, and local events of lay eucharistic preaching. These need to be positively presented as "favorable moments" (*kairoi*) and as authorized and supported safe transitional spaces with a proper theological and pastoral reflection mechanism. These experimentations are not about being sustainable throughout the church, all the time and everywhere, but about creating the occasions to question the normative standards (rooted in "sacrality") imposed to solve so-called pastoral problems. Lay eucharistic preaching is not to be reduced to a pastoral "problem" but be seen as a significant ecclesiological

du christianisme médiéval," *Les Cahiers du Centre de Recherches Historiques*, published online March 18, 2009, http://journals.openedition.org/ccrh/2798, DOI: https://doi.org/10.4000/ccrh.2798. One may also want to discover Hans Joas's *The Power of the Sacred: An Alternative to the Narrative of Disenchantment* (Oxford: Oxford University Press, 2021).

invitation by the Spirit to be attentive to the *semper reformanda* aspect of tradition (as a discourse) and the event of being the church of God in the world (as a practice).

As these experimentations do not mechanically generate enough energy for significant reform, these events should be accompanied by creating transformative relations between sacralized clergy and lay baptized women and men within parish settings and liturgical actions. For this to happen, revisions in how future priests are formed should be considered a priority. Also, the function of the laity ought to be presented as not restricted to the so-called secular sphere, as it is still too often.

Throughout this period and at the levels introduced previously, rhetorical choices should be made to avoid this experimentation being analyzed strictly from a logical or institutional perspective. Rhetoric here offers possibilities to create new affective circuits to foster adhesion to lay eucharistic preaching and debunk the effects that have constituted the subjection and damaging, mutilating effects of the current organization of the circulation of the Word in God's Church. This twofold rhetoric is required since the shaken confidence of many in the church and its present normativity concerning eucharistic preaching has become problematic.

Finally, the development of this playful rhetorical approach attentive to the socio-ecclesiological dimension of the theory and practice of lay eucharistic preaching is suggested to partially upset the effects that uncertainties always cause in any organization, ecclesial and secular. The uncertainties would come from the fact that some are troubled by the perturbation of the current separating principles of sacrality that define specific places, gestures, and possibilities for voicing opinions for different groups.

The advantages of an ecclesially grounded rhetorical practice are that it has the resources of metaphors, stories, and images to foster and generate theological hope that cannot be equated to a utopia and to encourage charitable *koinonia* as baptized men and women journey as the people of God, as the growing Body of Christ and as a temple of the Holy Spirit.

Something Must Be Ventured

Ruth Anne Henderson

> If any good thing shall go forward, something must be adventured.
>
> —Thomas More, *A Dialogue Concerning Heresies* (1529)

> Oh yes, I know you are all aware, in an abstract sort of way, that there is a substantial landmass called Europe near by. . . . If your concept of world geography was shaped entirely by what you read in the papers and saw on television, you would have no choice but to conclude that America must be about where Ireland is.
>
> —Bill Bryson, *Notes from a Small Island* (1995)

The British not only live on an island, but they have, as Bill Bryson suggests, an insular view of the rest of the world. Great Britain is, in fact, a part of the continent of Europe. The geographical facts are these: there are fifty countries in the European continent, some tiny but densely populated (e.g., Monaco, San Marino, Vatican City); Russia is by far the largest, at 2,881,250 square kilometers; the United Kingdom is less than one-tenth of that. The population density of the UK is 272 per square kilometer, of Italy 197, of France 123, of Germany

233, of the US a mere 37. These figures should be borne in mind when we consider the proposal that laypeople be authorized, after due training, to preach within the celebration of the Eucharist.

Less than half of European citizens identify as Roman Catholic; approximately 75 percent are nominally Christian, though church attendance is steeply declining in Western European countries, with Portugal being the only one with a substantial Catholic population. Despite the fact that the Vatican is in the heart of the Italian capital, Italy cuts a poor figure. Of the 80 percent or so of Italians who say they are Catholics, a mere quarter of that figure regularly attend Sunday Mass. Still less impressive is the state of the priesthood; in many European countries priests are often obliged to serve three or more parishes, with an effect on the faithful that can be imagined. An overworked cleric cannot be expected to serve his flock as his predecessors were able to do; and if, because of the pressure of his work, he has little time to prepare his homilies, they are unlikely to be inspiring. Nor is there any guarantee that seminarians, whose numbers are falling worldwide, will be offered the kind of preparation for preaching that is desirable—and for that matter, even the most fervent priest is not necessarily a gifted preacher.

In these circumstances, the collaboration of appropriately trained lay preachers is not only desirable but a matter of urgency. Not all churchgoing Catholics would be happy to listen to a layman or laywoman commenting on the day's gospel during the celebration of the Eucharist. So what about European lay Dominicans? We are members of the Order of Preachers. How do we preach, and what do we hope for as the fulfillment of our Dominican vocation?

It has to be admitted that lay Dominican formation tends, perhaps inevitably, to interpret preaching in terms that have little or nothing to do with the Eucharist. You preach with your life, we say—with your choices, with your response to criticism from family, friends, or acquaintances, with your conduct at work, and with how you occupy your free time. And yes, all this testifies (or at least should testify) to your commitment to the order and to the church; and not all lay Dominicans would be able (or willing) to deliver a homily in the course of Mass. However, some would gladly do so after attending special formation programs for lay preachers.

I asked fellow lay Dominicans from various parts of Europe—north, south, east, and west—to share their position on this topic. Regrettably, many failed to respond—none from northern or eastern countries; but those who did, without exception, said yes to the symposium's proposal to the synod. Some reported that they had been present when a person who was neither a priest nor a deacon delivered the homily—in some cases, a religious sister, in others, a representative of a charitable organization. Two responders hesitated, one because "this step should never be the first step towards women becoming priests or taking over other consecrated duties"—a possibility not even hinted at during the symposium. Another responder stressed "the years of study a priest has had before being considered learned enough to guide his flock." This is a reasonable observation, but how much of this study is devoted to the act of preaching—not only as it relates to theological content but also to relevance to the lives of the listeners and to delivery? Some intellectually gifted priests are poor communicators, sometimes all too evidently unprepared to deal with a microphone or inclined to mumble rather than enunciate clearly. I am thinking of English priests in particular; the English (not only priests) are notorious for their tendency to speak without moving their lips, as though practicing for a career as ventriloquists. (Scots, I am happy to report, are less inclined to this particular fault.) For people who are hard of hearing especially, this is a significant problem. If the congregation has difficulty in hearing or decoding what the preacher says, the homily, however theologically rich, will be a failure.

Another lay Dominican asked rhetorically, "Are there any characteristics of the sermon or homily that require it to be given by an ordained minister?" and offered the following response: "No. Every Christian is called to preach and announce the kingdom of God." This lay Dominican went on to emphasize that this is not authorization for any baptized persons to deliver a homily, saying, "If all baptized people can and should preach, not everyone will want to preach at the Eucharist; this requires that they be appointed, that they have this ministry. And the priest is already there for that. The question of who should preach was resolved by reserving this task to the priest. Not for essential reasons, but merely for practical ones." So how can the church move beyond this restrictive position, especially considering the decline in the numbers of priests and seminarians? As John Milton (1608–74) wrote in his poem *Lycidas*, "The hungry sheep look up, and are not fed." Properly trained—this is essential—lay preachers could help feed the hungry sheep.

A professor of theology who is also a lay member of the order offered the following reflection:

> How can we justify the participation of a lay person in the sacramental and liturgical framework assigned to an ordained minister? This question is crucial and

> fascinating. Here is my solution: We can justify such participation only if we seek to deepen the ecclesiology of Vatican II and Yves Congar. The ordained minister is undoubtedly the president of the sacrament, but the whole people of God celebrates the sacrament. The priest has the *potestas* to preside, but to preside for the people of God who celebrate the sacrament in their lay condition. The priest is the only president, but all the people (priest and laity) celebrate the sacrament of the Eucharist. Question: should the homily be the sole responsibility of the president (the ordained minister) or of the celebrants who constitute the whole people of God? If the homily could devolve to the celebrants (priest and people), the laity could participate in the homily. We must, therefore, insist on these two pillars: the priest in his *potestas* of president celebrates the sacrament; ontologically speaking, all the people of God celebrate the sacrament without the *potestas* of the presidency.

He offered a solution perfectly in line with the symposium's proposal: "The clerics could delegate it to lay people by an official act of appointment, or *even a ministry instituted in the same way as the ministry of the acolyte and reader.* I think the institution of such a ministry would be the solution: it guarantees the disciplinary position of the Church while including certain lay people duly instituted for this purpose" (italics mine).

A further contribution came from a member of the Dominican laity who has served on international councils over many years and has reflected at length on the role of the lay preacher:

> There are many religious sisters, nuns, and lay people who, due to their professional and human qualifications,

> would be in an excellent position to preach a good sermon. Many sisters and laypeople also have good basic theological knowledge; some have even studied theology, and some have the ecclesiastical teaching license *Missio Canonica*, but they all lack ordination. This lack of ordination is the only reason why they are excluded. As a result, the sermon is elevated to a kind of sacrament that only the ordained priest or deacon is authorized to give. This reasoning is no longer in keeping with the times and does not correspond to the texts from *Lumen Gentium*, which state that the faithful share in the prophetic ministry of Jesus Christ.

He added: "Especially when there is an increasing shortage of priests in Europe, it would be extremely desirable and important if lay people and sisters were more involved in liturgical services, including preaching. Their involvement would certainly be a blessing for the whole church!"

What is particularly striking in these responses is the recurrent reference to the Second Vatican Council, which has been under attack in recent years by the traditionalist wing of the church. Understandably, some worshipers feel a nostalgic longing for the preconciliar Church—for the Mass in Latin, for the elaborate ceremonial that is no longer a regular feature of our celebrations. The present writer, a postconciliar Catholic (with sufficient Latin to be able to follow the liturgy in that language but happy to participate in the vernacular), is persuaded that Cardinal Carlo Maria Martini was acknowledging an indisputable truth when he said, shortly before his death in 2012: "The Church is two hundred years behind the times. Why doesn't it shake itself up? Are we afraid? Afraid instead of courageous?"

The Synod on Synodality is a sign of courage in today's Church—courage to face our weaknesses, to seek solutions, and to innovate where necessary. The proposal that properly trained and officially authorized lay preachers be permitted to preach at the Eucharist is just such a courageous innovation. The most common phrase in the Bible is "Do not be afraid." Now, the church has an opportunity to show that we have heard and taken that invitation to heart.

Live and Proclaim the Word of God

Experiences in Lay Eucharistic Preaching from Germany

Kerstin-Marie Berretz

I studied theology from 1999 to 2004 at the Universities of Bochum and München. Nobody talked about the German exemption for lay eucharistic preaching in the 1970s and 1980s. We all knew that laypeople were not allowed to give the homily during the Eucharist, but we did not take it too seriously. So, when I attended a homiletic seminar at the Ludwigs-Maximilian-Universität in Munich in 2002, we did not hesitate to give our practice sermon in a parish during the Sunday Eucharist. We were happy that our teacher found a place for us students to preach.

However, only some were happy that laypeople gave the homily, and a fellow student discussed the situation with the professor of canon law. Consequently, the students of the following seminars had to preach during a Liturgy of the Word. This was my only experience when a report of a lay eucharistic preaching led to a consequence.

During my training as a pastoral assistant—a lay minister who works in a parish or a cluster of parishes as a specialized chaplain—in the Diocese of Treveris, we received our preaching training together with the young men preparing to become deacons and priests. We learned everything together, and when we were sent into parishes to have our first experiences in pastoral ministry, we became part of the preaching team for the Sunday Eucharist. I remember that the parish priest, who was my mentor, told the parish: "We all know that it is officially not allowed for a layperson to give the homily during the Eucharist. However, this situation is for educational reasons and only works if no one complains to the bishop."

We never heard that someone was unhappy with the lay preachings. On the contrary, various congregation members gave feedback on how much they appreciated the opportunity to listen to different preachers. So my colleague and I preached every second Sunday, Christmas, Good Friday, and on other occasions. At the end of the preaching training, an authorized bishop conducted the sermon examination during a weekday Eucharist after the gospel.

In 2007, after two and a half years of training, the bishop of the Diocese of Trier sent us four young pastoral assistants into service with the following words: "Live and proclaim the Word of God so his power may unfold in the hearts and lives of people."

And so it was pretty standard that we, as pastoral assistants, preached at the Eucharist, depending on where we worked. Proclaiming the Word of God was possible in the Diocese of Trier and several German dioceses where lay eucharistic preaching was and is a long-standing practice. For example, I preached on several occasions in the

Diocese of Essen, was invited to give a homily in Munich, and now regularly preach in my hometown, Vechta, in the Diocese of Münster.

I once recognized someone who photographed me while preaching in the Diocese of Essen. He afterward went to the sacristy to tell me that my sermon was against the law and that he wanted to report it to the responsible parish priest. The priest who had presided over the liturgy was not impressed by this statement, and the parish priest has yet to talk to me about the incident.

The bishop of Münster told me that he receives several reports on lay eucharistic preaching. Even though he does not see a problem with laypeople giving the homily, he understands the canon law and has to point out the legal situation. Nevertheless, it does not have any consequences for anybody.

However, that case shows the problematic situation in Germany. In several dioceses, it is a fact that lay ministers preach, and most of the people enjoy it. However, whether a trained person can preach depends on the priest and the bishop. There is no right to preach for lay ministers; so, as everywhere else in the world, if the priest is unwilling to let another person preach, there is no possibility. Even though people like to listen to a variety of preachers, and even though more people say that they enjoy a homily from a pastoral assistant than complain about it, and even though a person might have the talent to preach, it is always at the priest's discretion whether the person is allowed to preach.

That sometimes leads to the curious situation in which laypersons are not allowed to preach but their words may still be proclaimed in the Eucharist after the Gospel—as is the case when the preacher uses a published sermon template written by a layperson from a bimonthly sermon magazine. Around the world, ordained preachers can turn to print and online publications for sermons to be used for homily preparation or read as homilies during the Eucharist. No one knows that the ordained preacher is using a layperson's words to preach his homily.

At the same time, there is no legal certainty for a bishop or a priest who tolerates or allows lay eucharistic preaching. They are in a difficult situation, too. Thomas Schüller, professor of canon law at the University of Münster, points out that, besides the fact that nonordained preachers lack the right to preach, the bishops and priests can also receive legal complaints if they allow such preaching. Schüller also mentions that the 1973 *Directory for Masses with Children* is still valid and allows nonordained adults to preach at a Eucharist when children and adults celebrate together.[1] Hence, legalizing and welcoming lay eucharistic preaching is possible.

In light of all this, it is no surprise that lay eucharistic preaching was one of the topics of the Synodal Path of the German Catholic Church from 2020 to 2023. The bishops' conference designed the Synodal Path with the Central Committee of German Catholics (ZdK) to create formats for open debate and enable the responsible participation of women and men from all dioceses.

1. Congregation for Divine Worship, *Directory for Masses with Children* (Washington, DC: United States Catholic Conference, 1974) 24; Markus Nolte, "Kirchenrechtler: Predigtverbot für Laien ist nicht überzeugend [Canon Law Expert: Ban on Lay Preaching is Not Convincing]," *Kirche+Leben*, June 10, 2020, https://www.kirche-und-leben.de/artikel/kirchenrechtler-predigtverbot-fuer-laien-ist-nicht-ueberzeugend.

While listening and debating, the proclamation of the Gospel arose and led to an implementation text. This text, called "Proclamation of the Gospel by Authorised Baptised and Confirmed Persons in Word and Sacrament," was adopted by the synodal assembly on March 10, 2023.[2] As the title says, it deals with preaching by lay theologians and the cases of persons commissioned to preach who have not studied theology but are trained and commissioned to preach. It goes further than the previous debates about whether nonordained theologians should be allowed to preach. The members of the synodal assembly say in number 5:

> The German (Arch)bishops are seeking to boost the share of women and to increase diversity in the ministry of proclamation. In order to ensure the importance and improve the quality of the homily and to make better use of the richness of the manifold charisms, the German bishops should draw up a particular norm and obtain permission for this from the Holy See, according to which the homily can also be taken over in Eucharistic celebrations on Sundays and feast days by theologically and spiritually qualified faithful commissioned by the bishop, in accordance with the pastoral requirements recognized by the local Ordinary. A new Sermon Regulation would

2. Der Synodale Weg, "Handlungstext Verkündigung des Evangeliums durch beauftragte Getaufte und Gefirmte in Wort und Sakrament [Implementation Text: Proclamation of the Gospel by Authorised Baptised and Confirmed Persons in Word and Sacrament]," *Der Synodale Weg Nr. 12*, Bonn 2023, https://www.synodalerweg.de/fileadmin/Synodalerweg/Dokumente_Reden_Beitraege/beschluesse-broschueren/Englisch/SW-12_Proclamation-of-the-Gospel-by-authorised-baptised-and-confirmed-persons_Implementation-Text.pdf.

> set out more precise criteria for granting the authority to preach (facultas) and apply them to ordained and non-ordained preachers alike.

The Synodal Path thus does not ask for a change of canon law but a particular norm.

On June 22, 2023, the presidents of the Synodal Path, Bishop Georg Bätzing and Irme Stetter-Karp, informed Pope Francis of the results of the Synodal Path in a letter and officially presented him with the votes of the reform dialog. At the time of writing, there is no substantive response to the decisions of the Synodal Path, which may be due to the time overlap with the world synod.

Therefore, in 2024 the status quo in Germany is like this: In many dioceses, laypeople regularly preach on Sunday in the Eucharist after the gospel. Lay ministers receive preaching training on a very practical level. They are as well trained as priests and must pass an exam before the bishop sends them to their mission as pastoral assistants. Most of the people attending a Eucharist enjoy homilies from different preachers. They are grateful for the diverse insights into the Gospel. The perspectives of various preachers support the listening people in coming into contact with the Good News and make it easier to make correlations with life. At the same time, it is evident that some people do not enjoy lay eucharistic preaching, mainly because it is against the law.

Therefore, it would be helpful to legalize lay eucharistic preaching. The Synodal Path offered a possibility and a basis to anchor lay eucharistic preaching legally. The good experiences of lay eucharistic preaching show that it cannot be against the Holy Spirit and that it serves the proclamation of the Gospel.

Preacher as Midwife

Theresa Rickard

I have come to understand my evolving call as a preacher as being a midwife of the Word. The preacher does not possess the Word, but the Word possesses her as she listens attentively to the heartbeat of the people. She stands poised to react as she listens to stories of a community as they interface with the stories from the Bible and everyday life. The preacher accompanies the community as the community gives birth to the Word.

We find the image of midwife in several biblical accounts, including the well-known story of the two midwives, Shiphrah and Puah, in the Exodus event (Exod 1:15-22). These midwives disobey Pharaoh's order to kill Hebrew babies at birth. Instead, they courageously usher in life—saving Moses and other male infants. We also find God depicted metaphorically as a midwife in the Bible—God is the Creator and Sustainer of life. In Psalm 22, the psalmist is in danger and asks God to rescue him. "It was you [God] who took me from the womb; / you kept me safe on my mother's breast" (22:9).

A midwife assists a woman in giving birth. As a metaphorical midwife, a preacher assists a community in bringing forth something new—an insight, healing, forgiveness, or a new beginning. The midwife preacher accompanies and stands with the people, *naming the grace* already present and longing to be spoken.

The ministry of accompaniment becomes more important to me as my call to be preacher deepens. Accompaniment is essential to preaching an authentic word that resonates with the hearers. Pope Francis often writes and preaches on the art of accompaniment. In a general audience (Wednesday, January 4, 2023), he said: "He or she who accompanies does not substitute the Lord, does not do the work in the place of the person accompanied, but walks alongside him or her, encouraging them to interpret what is stirring in their heart, the quintessential place where the Lord speaks." The process of accompanying those who suffer or who need a listening ear or a helping hand is essential to my preaching life.

My authority to preach comes from my baptism, from being a vowed member of the worldwide Order of Preachers (Dominicans), and from recognition and affirmation by the community. Over forty years of public ministry, I have continued receiving invitations to preach in churches and retreat houses and at various liturgical events, including the Eucharist. Even though lay preaching is permitted in churches and oratories except at the Eucharist, Catholics are still surprised that women preach. In this synodal time, with the resounding call for women to assume greater leadership in the church and expand their ministerial impact, we can start by inviting women to preach at wake services, Liturgies of the Word, reconciliation services, and all appropriate church events. At the same time, we can advocate and pray for an outpouring of the Holy Spirit to expand the hearts and minds of synod participants to expand the instituted ministries of the church to include lay preacher—a commissioned ministry to preach at all liturgical services, including the Eucharist.

My vocation as a preacher began before I joined the Dominicans. In fact, my love of the Word of God and preaching drew me to the Dominicans. During my later college years, I experienced a profound outpouring of God's love and the Holy Spirit through my involvement in different Church renewal movements and campus ministry. After college, I was involved in various parish ministries and began to experience a call to full-time ministry. Lay ministry had only then started to flourish in the church. I attended a parish mission by a newly formed mission team composed of priests, sisters, and laypeople. It was a dynamic, creative, and life-changing ministry, and the church was filled. After experiencing this mission in my parish, I joined the Archdiocese of New York Parish Mission Team. It was my first experience of pulpit preaching. Mgr. James Conlan, the team director, was the best preacher I ever heard and a compassionate and dynamic minister. He did both preaching and accompaniment well. I caught the fire for preaching through his guidance and instruction and by living the apostolic life with him and the other team members. I spent three years with the mission team, traveling from parish to parish, preaching God's word through story and music. Two of the many lessons I learned from Fr. Jim: never be the hero of the story you share; and if you don't love the people in the pew, then you have no place in the pulpit. My preaching life began in an official church ministry that recognized my gift, honed my homiletic skills, and willingly shared the pulpit with me and my colleagues. Living in a praying community and preaching from that experience led me to enter the Dominican Sisters.

However, I was young and naive and had no idea this was a unique ministry at a creative time in the church. I assumed the church would welcome my preaching gift, which so many listeners had affirmed. Primarily through the support of my Dominican sisters and brothers, God continued to open doors to my preaching ministry despite restrictions on women preachers and despite struggles throughout the years. I acknowledge that being a vowed Dominican woman gave me more theological education, more opportunities to preach, and more support to keep preaching than my lay counterparts often have. I wish all women the same opportunities. I am committed to supporting and accompanying lay preachers.

My preaching life continued to grow through my formation as a Dominican sister, formal theological study, and dedication to the apostolic life. After professing vows as a Dominican, I ministered as a pastoral associate at a vibrant, multicultural, and multilingual parish in the Bronx, New York. The pastoral team shared the ministry of the Word, which included preaching at Sunday Eucharist. I began preaching monthly at the Masses conducted in English. Although I had some facility in Spanish, I did not feel prepared to preach a homily in that language. At the same time, I began a small Christian community of Spanish-speaking women. The group grew in number and faith as we gathered weekly for faith sharing on the Sunday Scriptures. The small community named itself Las Damas Bíblicas en Acción (Biblical Women in Action).

After a few months, the women asked me why I was not preaching at the Spanish Mass. I explained, "I don't feel ready." They responded, "¡Estamos listas!" (We are ready!) When my turn to preach in Spanish came, we prepared the homily together. I developed an oral manuscript from our faith sharing; one woman corrected it, and my dear friend Evelyn practiced with me for hours. The first Sunday I preached, Las Damas Bíblicas came out in force. At the end of my homily, they stood up and clapped, and the whole community joined in. It was not my homily but ours—it came forth from the community and resonated with them. I was not the only one empowered that day to share my God-given gifts. As Layla A. Karst explains in one of her arguments for lay eucharistic preaching, my authority to preach did not come from sacramental ordination but from my public ministry with the people.

My desire to share the Word of God with a larger audience led me to ministry at RENEW International. I spent twenty years ministering at RENEW, developing small Christian communities in parishes worldwide. The purpose of small communities is the same as the homily—to help a community connect scriptural meaning with their lived experience and form a vivid dialogue between text and life to forge contemporary Christian praxis. I continued pulpit preaching while empowering laypeople to engage in the preaching conversation in small communities.

At this synodal moment, we are standing at the birthstool of a new community. This community recognizes and shares all the gifts of the baptized, especially that the Word of God might be preached and heard more effectively. We, both the ministerial priesthood and the priesthood of the faithful, are called to be midwives, ushering in a renewed and revitalized Church in this new time and context. We need bold and Spirit-filled preaching from both clerical and lay preachers for the sake of the mission of the church.

Eucharistic Preachers Modeling a Generous God

Deborah Wilhelm

> And he told them many things in parables, saying: "Listen! A sower went out to sow. And as he sowed, some seeds fell on the path, and the birds came and ate them up. Other seeds fell on rocky ground, where they did not have much soil, and they sprang up quickly, since they had no depth of soil. But when the sun rose, they were scorched; and since they had no root, they withered away. Other seeds fell among thorns, and the thorns grew up and choked them. Other seeds fell on good soil and brought forth grain, some a hundredfold, some sixty, some thirty. Let anyone with ears listen!"
> —Matthew 13:3-9

Jesus Returns: An Updated Version of the Parable of the Sower

Imagine that Jesus is on his way back to earth right this minute, and the first thing he says when he gets here is this: "Sorry, gang, but I've had to amend one of those parables that I told you back in my early days. So listen now to the 'Parable of the Sower 2.0': *Once a sower went out to sow some seeds. Some of them fell on the path, some on rocky ground, and some among thorns. The sower looked around, and remembering that the good seed is costly, he clenched his seeds in his fist and decided to plant elsewhere next year.*"

In my home garden, I'm ever mindful of the cost of seeds. They're expensive, small, easily lost. If I stumble while the little paper seed packet is open, the entire precious cargo becomes instant lunch for the finches, sparrows, and jays of the Willamette Valley. Even the seeds that I save myself from year to year are expensive, just in a different way. Like sowers of old, I plan for the future by letting some plants mature past harvest, collecting their seeds, drying them, and trying to package them safely from the predations of mold and winter bugs. However, whether purchased or homegrown, the effort to get seeds into the ground is considerable. So I guard them jealously, like the seed caster in "Parable of the Sower 2.0."

"Sower 2.0" is patently ridiculous, of course. It's unhopeful, graceless. It leaves out the best parts. Where's the good soil that yields a rich harvest, prominently featured in "Sower 1.0 (Jesus' Version)"? More importantly, where is the generosity of the seed caster? And yet, "Sower 2.0" seems like an apt metaphor for my experience as a preacher and a hearer of preaching.

Everyone has heard the depressing statistics about how awful Catholic preaching is, how preaching is one of the reasons that Catholics are leaving for other faith communities, how preaching alienates many groups of believers, how preaching fails to communicate our tradition or speak to our lives, so I won't belabor those. Research results like these raise significant concerns but are not the topic here. Rather than speak from scarcity, I want to speak toward abundance, the as-yet-unrealized potential of a synodal church in mission.

I come to this essay with a specific hermeneutic based on my social location, with a text formed through that lens. Here it is: as someone who is called as a preacher, who holds a doctorate in preaching, who teaches preaching, who has preached at Eucharist, *and* who is a layperson, I have listened to every kind of preaching and have asked, *How can the preaching at our eucharistic liturgies help God's word to take root, grow, thrive, and yield a harvest?*

The question is deceptively simple, but "Sower 1.0 (Jesus' Version)" helps us to explore it. I did not grow up in good soil (a story for another time), so my very life testifies to God's generous seed sowing, to the truth that even a seed sown in the most unlikely place might sprout. This is also true of my preaching life. I was Catholic in name only until, in young adulthood, I returned, tentatively, to practicing the faith of my heritage. I was teaching technical writing to engineering majors at a large public university, and contentedly so. But one particular day, sitting in a preaching class with a group of deacon candidates (one of whom is my husband) and their wives, the Holy Spirit whispered to me. I opened my ears but said nothing. As happens, the Spirit kept bothering me, touching my mind and heart, and I kept saying "No, thanks" until finally I said, "Okay, maybe."

Eventually, those maybes shifted toward yes. And the church confirmed the call. Professors said, "There's a gift here." Colleagues said, "There's a gift here." The bishop said, "There's a gift here." (He later retired, and the bishop who came next said the same thing.) My pastor said, "There's a gift here, and it's my responsibility to nurture that gift." (He later retired, and the pastor who came next said the same thing.) My parish family said, "Thank you." It took an entire community and much work, as it should, before I could come to the ambo. But Spirit and Church called me forward.

Then the Dominicans took me in, accepting me for doctoral study and forming me in a charism I barely knew I had. They taught me to see myself not as a person who happens to preach but as a preacher. Like the work of acquiring good seed, this process was expensive, both literally and figuratively. But again, I found myself helped forward. My bishop and I wrote a preaching book together. I developed a preaching curriculum for graduate study at a Catholic university. I preached at Eucharist every Friday and one weekend every other month, coming to the ambo from my seat in the assembly among the worshiping community and returning to that seat afterward.

Those days of blessing and generosity affirmed the labor and expense, but they ended abruptly for me with a move to a new diocese where only clergy speak at public prayer. So these days, I'm a preacher in the pews, longing for a transformative word to reach my ears, longing to speak a transformative word to the people among whom I sit. Instead, I experience absence—not the nourishing silence that cradles a word heard or spoken, but simply a void, an aching emptiness.

Why emptiness? In my current parish, many people know that I'm a preacher and a homiletician, and some follow my online preaching, and a few read my publications. Still, I have no local liturgical presence as a preacher. One weekend a month, my husband (a deacon) preaches at Mass, and I listen from my place in the pew. Once or twice a year, I'm invited to fill in for a missing lector. Occasionally, if there's a shortage of ministers for a particular liturgy, I'm asked to help take up the collection or to carry the cross in the procession. And I'm happy to do these things. But the Holy Spirit who called me as a preacher years ago still calls me now, and I feel it keenly. These days, especially at Eucharist, hearing that voice brings pain and sorrow. So before we move on, I will say right here that this suffering is real and ongoing. Also, I am not alone.

Scarcity: Preachers and Listeners

We are suffering from a hermeneutic of scarcity. It seems that the preached Word at Eucharist is being held—needlessly—in a closed fist, much as I might protect my garden seeds. The generous sowing of God's word feels threatened, with clergy citing scarcity of time, energy, and preparation because of the continual encroachment of other, more urgent, ministerial demands. Distressingly, I also hear blame cast about. You may have heard or perhaps even said some of these things yourself: people don't know how to pay attention anymore; the culture is too secular; social media have degraded communication into a caricature of itself; Catholics are undercatechized or miscatechized. The list is long. The language of blame is found even in some of our documents.[1] This line of

1. See, for example, the USCCB's *Preaching the Mystery of Faith*, which laments "that many Catholics, for a variety of reasons, seem either indifferent to or disaffected with the Church and her teaching" (United States Conference of Catholic Bishops, *Preaching the*

thinking doesn't help. It argues that if the Word of God isn't growing in people's lives, they have mostly themselves to blame.

These are important concerns, but here I also want to focus on a different kind of scarcity that touches upon the preaching call per se: the opinion that many or most of the people of God gathered at Mass are "only there for the Eucharist." This "only there for the Eucharist" idea creates an artificial and destructive liturgical scarcity in our thought and practice. Preaching at Eucharist, the thinking goes, can be spotty, but we can accept that since we're really just there for the Eucharist. One popular Catholic speaker, the author of (at last count) some thirty books, is direct in his dismissal of eucharistic preaching: "When we go to Mass on Sunday the danger is in thinking that the music and the homily are the most important things. *Don't take the trivial and make it important.*"[2] Ideas like these impoverish our liturgies and undermine our liturgical theology. Nobody's likely to argue that the music and the homily are the "most important things." But not being the "most important" doesn't make them trivial, nor does it diminish in any way their actual importance.

The Liturgy of the Word and the Liturgy of the Eucharist together form "one single act of worship."[3] They're

---

Mystery of Faith: The Sunday Homily [Washington, DC: USCCB, 2012], 4). The bishops mention the sexual abuse crisis, but the list of critiques is mostly aimed at contemporary people as members of contemporary culture: individualism, consumerism, racism, and relativism are offered as findings from "recent studies" (4–5).

2. Matthew Kelly, ed., introduction to *Beautiful Eucharist* (Wellspring, 2023), 3; emphasis added.

3. *Sacrosanctum Concilium* ("Constitution on the Sacred Liturgy" [SC]) 56.

not to be divided, one from another, into less-important and more-important. Worshipers who are "only there for the Eucharist" might think that they're getting the "important" half of the liturgy, but this separation means that they're not getting a eucharistic liturgy, period. Yes, homiletic quality ranges from quite bad to quite good and everywhere in between. But every eucharistic liturgy deserves—demands, even—good preaching, good seeds generously sown.

Generosity: Church and Spirit

How might the spirit of generosity inform Catholic preachers and preaching? Long ago, a friend who is an experienced Catholic priest and professor spoke to me of his compassion for persons who are called to ministry but do not receive ecclesial commissioning. He said the only insight he could offer was to tell people living in this tension, "Yes, perhaps God is calling you. But right now, the church is not."

He would say these words kindly, and they made a sort of sense—at first, anyway. But they ultimately fail, because the church *is* indeed calling laypeople to preach. I have seen the Word of God, proclaimed and interpreted by lay preachers at Eucharist, sown and grown in community. As listeners hearing "Sower 1.0 (Jesus' Version)," we're accustomed to asking ourselves what kind of soil we are. But another question for the church is to ask ourselves what kinds of sowers we are. Do we, the church, sow God's word with God's generosity? Or, rather, are we doing what I've been doing with my garden seeds, clenching the Word tightly in a fist instead of casting it over the earth? Are we overlooking persons who are gifted, formed, and affirmed by the Holy Spirit and their communities, needlessly dividing clergy and laity in the shared task of proclamation and interpretation?

The eucharistic homily is the only preaching that most Catholics ever experience and is a privileged moment of communication. In the Mass, almost every word or movement is scripted, written in our missals and rubrics, attended to with care, and occasionally even "policed" by ministers or assembly members. In our corporate worship, we know when to stand, sit, and kneel, how to hold (or not hold) our hands, what to sing, what to speak. We teach our lectors not to alter so much as a word of the introduction to the readings ("A reading from the book of Genesis" rather than "This morning's first reading comes from the book of Genesis," for example) because even that little phrase is written in the lectionary with purpose. Our music comes from approved songbooks. One exception to this scriptedness comes in the prayers of the faithful, especially in parishes that still permit the faithful to speak aloud their own prayers after the community prayers are read. But the main exception, the one place in which vernacular words become seeds sown in human lives, and the only place in which interpretation is actively encouraged, is the homily.

Lay Eucharistic Preaching: The Holy Spirit, Vision, Will, and Wisdom

What are we supposed to do now? you may well be thinking here. We need the Spirit. We need vision. We need will. We need a generous wisdom. In our work at the lay eucharistic preaching symposium, we practiced these things to show what can happen when people come together in trust for conversation across potentially contentious lines. We made synodal listening our model. After preliminary research and study, we gathered. We prayed together. We listened together for the Holy Spirit before anyone spoke. We paused regularly to listen again. Every person in the room spoke from their own experience, knowledge, social location, and insight. We ate, sang, prayed the Hours, and celebrated Eucharist together. We asked the Holy Spirit to sow wisdom among us and to tend us, body, soul, and spirit, each of us individually and all of us together.

We became rich, fertile soil, willing to make the case—theologically, liturgically, ministerially, and ecclesially—for lay preaching at Eucharist. The fruits of that work appear in detail elsewhere in this collection. But preaching is also a personal and vocational concern. My story here is simultaneously particular and general. Every preacher everywhere has a vocation story. We come to this moment as preachers, lay and ordained, to whom the Spirit of God has whispered, "Preach. Become sowers so that my Word can flourish." *We make the case for lay eucharistic preaching not as a critique of clergy preaching nor a solution to the preaching crisis but because Scripture, tradition, and our own experience support it.* What would the world look like if we, the church, sowed the seeds of God's word as generously as God does? A synodal church in mission—a faith-filled, believing Church that listens to the Spirit—calls forth such sowers. The good, costly seed comes best from the open hand.

Prophetic Protagonists Anointed by the Spirit

Wayne Cavalier

It happened on more than one occasion. In fact, it became a regular occurrence. At the time, I supported my stipend for a newly created role on our Dominican leadership team by spending half my time working with Isaiah Missions. We preached parish missions and simultaneously begged for sponsors and donations to the Christian Foundation for Children and Aging (now Unbound).[1] Sue Blum, a lay adult convert to Catholicism, ran Isaiah Missions. We used a team approach to preaching—usually a laywoman, but sometimes a non-ordained religious, teamed up with a priest.

The "it" moment was always after the final Mass of the mission. A congregation member would approach me (the ordained preacher) and say: "When I saw her get up to preach, I was against it. But after hearing her, I'm a believer!"

I am a believer, too. It did not take much for me to get there. My vocation is often tied up with the false notion

1. See https://www.unbound.org/.

that only ordained ministers can nourish God's people with the Word of God at the eucharistic feast. The same priest who inspired my vocation—by his intelligence, compassion, wisdom, steadfast but unassuming faith, and general competence—convinced me of a simple truth: ordination does not necessarily give one the gift of preaching. I loved and admired him, but he could not preach. Sitting in the pew on any given Sunday, I would grow sad and frustrated at how poorly nourished my fellow Mass-goers were at the homily time.

Furthermore, this priest knew this about himself. It must have been torture. I would sit there thinking, "Even I could do better than this!" Five years later, I entered the Order of Preachers, better known as the Dominicans.

In this essay, I argue that our goal at the eucharistic table should be to nourish God's people before sending them on mission. The Eucharist is the "summit and source" for the rest of our lives, out there. Because of the vital importance of this sacrament in our lives, we should not put artificial and unnecessary strictures around feeding God's people with the living Word. Keeping the current limitations on preaching in the eucharistic context is unnecessary and risks adequate nourishment of the Body of Christ for its mission.

Priestly Ordination and Preaching

I grew up in a household strongly identified as practicing Catholic, surrounded by a historically Franco-Iberian Catholic culture in southern Louisiana. As I went to college, the first in my family to do so, I began to associate with a more diverse crowd, though still religious. Bill, a Presbyterian with a winning personality, loved to pray with the Bible regularly. He challenged me once as a Catholic, charging that I probably grew up in a house that didn't even have a Bible in it.

The next time I saw my Mom, I asked her. She said indignantly, "Of course we have a Bible!"

"Where is it?" It was an honest question.

"It's on the top shelf of the closet in your sisters' room—in the back," she said. She got quiet and said, "We were told we should not read the Bible because only the priest could correctly interpret it."

This Catholic conviction, remotely rooted in a reaction to the baptismal and biblical emphases of the Reformation, is no doubt foundational to the restrictions related to who can interpret the Word of God for the congregation in the context of the eucharistic liturgy. A whole theological justification surrounds it. Could it be that this inherited state of affairs is as misguided as the remoteness of the Word of God is to the daily lives of many Catholics, founded on an outdated historical reaction shored up by impressive-sounding theological justifications?

In the fifteenth century, the invention of the printing press made broad access to the Word of God possible. As more people put their hands on the Bible, they began to read it and interpret it for themselves. Broader access to education and Bible reading became a threat to clerical power.[2]

2. See, for example, Joshua J. Mark, "The Printing Press and the Protestant Reformation," *World History Encyclopedia*, July 18, 2022, https://www.worldhistory.org/article/2039/the-printing-press--the-protestant-reformation/.

Today's Catholic community is the most educated in the church's history.[3] Not only is this true of the Catholic population in general, but it is especially true regarding advanced theological knowledge. Laypeople now study theology and Scripture, and pastoral teams commonly include lay ministers with the same or more education in Scripture and preaching as ordained ministers. At many seminaries, women professors, lay and religious, are forming seminarians (and others) in their knowledge and interpretation of Scripture. In a few of those seminaries, women teach future priests to preach.[4]

With the conviction promoted by Yves Congar, OP, among others, and wholly adopted at the Second Vatican Council, that the sacraments of initiation offer all the faithful a share in the priestly, prophetic, and kingly ministry of Christ in carrying on his mission,[5] the role of the ordained strikes a different key than perhaps might

3. See Justin Nortey, Patricia Tevington, and Gregory A. Smith, "9 Facts about U.S. Catholics," Pew Research Center, April 12, 2024, https://pewrsr.ch/3VRqirS.

4. See, for example, Elise Ann Allen, "Female Theologians Back Ouellet: Seminaries Need Women Involved in Formation," *Crux*, May 11, 2020, https://cruxnow.com/interviews/2020/05/female-theologians-back-ouellet-seminaries-need-women-involved-in-formation/. See also University of Dallas, "Institute for Homiletics in Catholic Church Established in North Texas: Pioneer in Listener Studies from University of Notre Dame, Karla J. Bellinger, Selected as Founding Executive Director," news release, September 14, 2024, https://news.udallas.edu/09-14-21-Institute-for-Homiletics-in-Catholic-Church-Established-in-North-Texas.

5. See Yves Congar, *The Mystery of the Church* (Baltimore: Helicon Press, 1960), 128–45, 182–87, and Yves Congar, *Lay People in the Church: A Study for a Theology of Laity*, trans. Donald Attwater (Westminster, MD: Newman Press, 1959.), 115.

have been required when there was a real danger of the undereducated laity seriously misinterpreting the Word of God. No longer is it necessary to burden the role either of the ordained or of the eucharistic presider with solely representing the person of Christ in the worship of the community. This conviction led Congar to conclude that all the baptized members of the Body of Christ are the protagonists or subjects of the eucharistic action.[6]

This insight opens new vistas on the liturgical action for the whole community—that is, the one Body of Christ—and what role each can play in the liturgical action. In that action, the entire body partakes of the mystery that identifies each with Christ and sends each to embody effectively Christ's continuing mission in the world.

This theological understanding goes hand in hand with contemporary pastoral reality in many places. Although some aspects of that reality have always been part of the Catholic experience in the United States, the pastoral reality differs from one part of the country to another and from one Catholic community to the next. Indeed, it is often different for distinct cultural and ethnic communities that belong to the same Catholic parish, pastored by one priest frequently with pastoral responsibility spread over several parish communities.

In some regions, the church is in decline. There are fewer ordinations and fewer parishioners. Yet, given that there are many historically established parish communities

6. See Yves Congar, "The *Ecclesia* or Christian Community as a Whole Celebrates the Liturgy," in *At the Heart of Christian Worship: Liturgical Essays of Yves Congar*, trans. and ed. Paul Philibert (Collegeville, MN: Liturgical Press, 2010).

whose members do not want to or cannot pragmatically let go of their parish location, ordained ministers are stretched to serve multiple parishes at different locations.

In other places, the Catholic population is growing. This growth is unprecedented in the number of Catholics present and the relative size of the Catholic population compared to what pastoral resources are available to serve their needs. The ratio of parishioners to ordained ministers has grown exponentially in a relatively brief period.[7] Dramatically outnumbered ordained ministers are stretched thin caring for large congregations, sometimes at multiple sites.

Immigration also is a factor. The declining number of ordained ministers our country has experienced almost everywhere means that the burden of learning how to minister interculturally falls precisely on the shoulders of those whose pastoral burden is increasing. Ordained pastors are stretched across multiple parishes and expected to minister to growing numbers of parishioners with whom they may not have a shared cultural or ethnic background, religious practices, or language.

These situations set ordained ministers up for failure on many fronts. Preaching requires contemplative space to pray with Scripture, research to understand the readings in their context, time for homily preparation, and understanding of the community so that the preacher may assist the community in responding to the Word of God in its context. Instead, most priests who do ministry

7. See, for example, Crux Staff, "New Study Shows Changes in the U.S. Catholic Church over Past 50 Years," *Crux*, April 5, 2024, https://cruxnow.com/church-in-the-usa/2024/04/new-study-shows-changes-in-the-u-s-catholic-church-over-past-50-years.

across several parish communities have little time to get to know the members of each community and the realities those members deal with day in and day out. These pastors have little contemplative space to encounter the Word of God at a spiritual level. They often do not have the time needed to craft effective homilies. Furthermore, while many priests in intercultural ministries go to heroic lengths to gain skills to communicate with and offer pastoral care in their parishioners' languages, only the rare priest can attain the ability to overcome entirely the language and cultural barriers they face.

In such cases, I believe it is a sin to offer such poor nourishment when a much richer offering may be possible by admitting to the preaching ministry laity with the vocation and formation to preach. While limiting the interpretation of the Word of God to priests made sense when they were the only people with the education and preparation to carry out this ministry, that is not the case in many places today.

Instead, the church must imagine a situation in which the pastor-presider can preside over the Liturgy of the Word without necessarily having to deliver the homily himself. As lay lectors proclaim the Word in the first and second readings, and music ministers lead the responsorial psalm and alleluia verse, so trained and instituted lay preachers could preach the homily. The congregation can thus receive nourishment from a preacher who knows the community's ways and language and has spent sufficient time with God's word without sacrificing pastoral care or parochial administration. Such rich nourishment prepares the faithful to say amen to communion with their Lord and strengthens the Body of Christ for mission.

Too many congregations suffer through ineffective preaching today while gifted lay preachers sit in the pews with tears in their eyes, thinking, "Even I could do better than this!"

Setting the Question in a Dominican Context

Gregory Heille

Several nonordained vowed religious and associates see preaching as integral to their religious institute's charism and their vocation. Conversations among women and men over the years in the Order of Preachers are relevant to this discernment about a pastoral charge for lay preaching at the Eucharist.

In 1982, a year before the 1983 Code of Canon Law was enacted, the Dominican Leadership Conference in the United States hosted a conference on preaching and the nonordained in Columbus, Ohio. The conference papers edited by Nadine Foley, OP, in a 1983 volume called *Preaching and the Non-Ordained: An Interdisciplinary Study* were the first record of a significant dialogue about lay preaching in the Order of Preachers.[1]

1. Nadine Foley, ed., *Preaching and the Non-Ordained: An Interdisciplinary Study* (Collegeville, MN: Liturgical Press, 1983). Contributors included Nadine Foley, OP, Kathleen Cannon, OP, Edward Schillebeeckx, OP, Sandra Schneiders, IHM, William J. Hill, OP, Mary Collins, James H. Provost, and Joan Delaplane, OP.

Years later, in a statement titled "Men and Women in Mission Together," the delegates at the 1998 General Chapter of Dominican Friars in Bologna, Italy, affirmed that "Lay men and women offer a unique vision of preaching and living the Gospel because of their total insertion into society with all of its secular, economic, and political realities."[2] The delegates went on to say the following:

> We encourage Dominicans from all branches of the Order to claim their identity as preachers. Furthermore, we ask all members to prepare themselves for this preaching and to take advantage of every opportunity. We are aware that the exclusion of women from ordained ministry and consequently from preaching the homily at the Eucharist is a painful experience for many. At the same time we are also aware that the debate itself on the ordination of women is painful for many. While remaining respectful of the Church's *Magisterium*, we are convinced that our Order is called to find creative ways to release the fullness of our preaching charism. We owe it to *Veritas*—the Dominican goal of truth—to advance the theological and ecclesiological dimensions of this question.[3]

2. Acts of the General Chapter of the Order of Friars Preachers, Bologna (1998) 34.4. This section of the essay draws from a seven-page unpublished report submitted in September 2004 by Gregory Heille, OP, and Mary Jean Traeger, OP, to the Dominican Leadership Conference Preaching Committee, titled "Background with Respect to the Order's Theological Commission on the Charism of Preaching for Women and Men of the Order of Preachers and Its Report to the Master of the Order dated May 2001."

3. Acts of the General Chapter, Bologna (1998) 34.6.

The Bologna chapter petitioned the Master of the Order of Preachers "*to constitute a commission of highly competent theologian brothers and sisters of the Order, whose task will be to examine the question of the charism of preaching for men and women of the Order and its relation to ordained ministry, and to advance the theological and ecclesiological dimensions of the question.*"[4] The Theological Commission on the Charism of Preaching for Women and Men in the Order of Preachers began meeting in March 2000 and submitted its final report in May 2001 to the order's curia in Rome. The commission's 2001 report said in its opening that the "Order of Preachers has a privileged mandate to preach God's word by its very nature."[5] The report stated, "As an Order with a centuries-long tradition of membership of both men and women, we Dominicans have the opportunity and a particular responsibility to respond to the 'signs of the times' relative to cultural and social change inclusive of women in leadership and prophetic insight." The report went on to state:

4. Acts of the General Chapter, Bologna (1998) 42. Timothy Radcliffe, OP, appointed Sister Mary Catherine Hilkert (professor of theology at University of Notre Dame, Akron Dominicans), Sister Mary O'Driscoll (professor of spirituality at the Angelicum, Cabra Dominicans of Ireland), Sister Benedicta Hintersberger (professor of theology at the Dominican Sisters' Academy, Dominican Convent of St. Ursula, Augsburg, Germany), Friar Hervé Legrand (professor of ecclesiology, Institut Catholique, Paris), and Friar Paul Philibert (prior of St. Dominic Priory, St. Louis, and chairperson for the commission).

5. Quotations are taken from the nine-page unpublished final report of the Commission titled "The Dominican Charism of Preaching: An Inquiry (May 2001)."

> Pastoral experience with diverse ministers of the Word has led an increasing number of communities and persons to question why the Eucharistic homily, as the preeminent preaching of the Church, is restricted to ordained males. (Carlo Molari wrote in the early 1970s: "[T]he content [of the announcement of the gospel] emerges only through the experience of the gospel which believers have lived out in their different life situations through the action of the Spirit. For this reason the fact that only the priest comments on the scripture readings and unveils their present-day meaning is not sufficient for the authentic proclamation of the Word of God today.")[6]

The report asked that several theological concerns be addressed: the relationship between the ministerial priesthood and the common priesthood of the baptized, the connection between charism and office, the pastoral concern that the Word of God is preached and heard more effectively, and how canon law relates to pastoral practice.

Though the curia submitted the report to the 2001 General Chapter in Providence, the chapter did not review it or give it constitutional status. It seemed to commission chairperson Paul Philibert that different readers interpreted the document and its agendas differently, according to their social location and agendas. The concern from the United States about women being allowed to preach at the Eucharist was not the principal concern of Dominicans from other parts of the world. The report did not go as far as some commission members

6. Carlo Molari, *La Fede e il suo linguaggio* (Assisi: Cittadella Editrice, 1972), 280–84. Translation by John Dunn.

wished and went further than others hoped in terms of making a positive practical-pastoral response to Vatican policy prohibiting lay liturgical preaching and in terms of making a theological rationale for lay preaching in the church by profession into the Dominican charism. These concerns may explain why the document never reached discussion at the General Chapter of Providence.

The Preaching Commission at the 2004 General Chapter of Cracow, which included the former Master of the Order Timothy Radcliffe, OP, studied the report of the Theological Commission chaired by Paul Philibert, OP, and encouraged wide discussion among the Dominican family on two questions: "Is collaborative preaching by Dominican women and men, lay and ordained, essential to our witness to the gospel?" and "How does profession in the Order of Preachers imply a commission to preach as a participation in the essential mission of the Order?" The chapter recommended that "before the next chapter a small meeting of theologians, historians, pastors, and canonists be held to evaluate responses, continue the reflection, and propose future steps to be taken."[7]

In the view of Philibert, the obvious obstacle to further canonical progress in this area was the stagnation that settled upon the Vatican during the period of Pope John Paul II's serious illness. Cardinal Castrillon-Hoyos, prefect of the Congregation for the Clergy, commented in releasing the 1997 "Instruction on Certain Questions Regarding the Collaboration of the Non-Ordained Faithful in the Sacred Ministry of Priest" that the instruction

7. Acts of the General Chapter of the Order Friars Preachers, Cracow (2004) 58.

intended to address "the secularization of the clergy and the clericalization of the laity," which prohibited lay homiletic preaching. Cardinal Francis Arinze, prefect of the Congregation for Divine Worship and the Discipline of the Sacraments from 2002 to 2008, was convinced that the reclericalization of the ordained—giving them status, dignity, and authority—was the solution to vocation recruitment and the return of order to a church that had become overlocalized. According to Philibert's view, personal preferences notwithstanding, only two effective avenues are open to us to make progress on the question of reviving and extending the charism of preaching: (1) the exercise of collaborative preaching of the faithful with the ordained in canonically acceptable contexts (or at least marginally so in the light of *Redemptionis Sacramentum*) such as parish renewals, retreats, catechetical preaching, or evangelization; and (2) continued theological work on the charism of preaching in the church and its link to the prophetic charism of baptismal priesthood—and perhaps some deconstructive work on the imposing but fundamentally wrong force of the idea of the "laity" as a second-tier "people of God."

At the 2022 general chapter of the Dominican friars in Tultenango, Mexico, the delegates made a statement about the preaching mission of the Dominican family that seems aligned with the first of these two paths: "Though the whole Dominican Family has been given this task, we each fulfill it according to our own particular role in the Body of Christ: the laity preach differently than the nuns, the friars differently from the apostolic sisters. And among the friars, the cooperator brothers and priests also preach in distinct ways. Each of these roles is unique; and as the mouth needs the lungs to speak, and the lungs need the mouth to breathe, so each part of the Dominican Family needs each other for Christ's preaching to be complete."[8] The delegates explicitly supported the church's canonical stance on lay preaching: "The beginning of a clarification of their mandate for preaching is to point out that they have received that mandate in virtue of their Baptism. It can be pointed out, secondly, that there are formal and informal ways of preaching. The laity are not expected to prepare homilies."[9]

The Tultenango chapter also made a broad appeal for synodality in the church: "If we as Dominicans are to preach the Gospel effectively, we must walk together (*syn-*) along the Way (*odos*) which is Christ the Preacher (cf. Jn 14:6)."[10] Perhaps a synodal path allows for reconsidering the second of the two paths, as given above.

8. Acts of the General Chapter of the Order of Friars Preachers, Tultenango (2022) 78.

9. Acts of the General Chapter, Tultenango 129.

10. Acts of the General Chapter, Tultenango 79.

Catholic Women Preach

Raising Voices, Renewing the Church

Elizabeth A. Donnelly

From 1981 to 1983, I served as a Maryknoll Lay Missioner in Lima, Peru, and witnessed firsthand the devastating impact of the economic crisis on my friends and neighbors there. I returned to the United States as an enthusiastic student of Catholic social thought. I researched extensively and interviewed policymakers in Washington and Europe about the Catholic Church's contribution to the global campaign for debt relief for heavily indebted countries to free up money for health and education.

I interviewed amazing, dedicated people like Senator Bill Bradley of New Jersey. Almost to a person they said that the Catholic Church's credibility in addressing an international issue like the debt crisis arose from the fact that it was Catholic laity, women religious, and clergy who were accompanying the poorest of the poor around the world. And yet the church's credibility was undermined by the church's stance on several issues, not the least of which was its treatment of women as second-class members—and this was before the sexual abuse crisis came to widespread recognition.

The experience strengthened my resolve to join others to elevate women's leadership roles in the church and fully recognize and deploy Catholic women's ample gifts for the common good.

My family has a small Catholic foundation based in Pittsburgh, where I grew up. Because of that, we have been extremely fortunate to be longtime members of Foundations and Donors Interested in Catholic Activities, a philanthropic network of approximately fifty-five foundations and various asset-sized donors supporting Catholic activities and initiatives.

In 2007, one of our European members with deep ties at the Vatican invited several women to engage in dialogue with senior curia officials on the role of women in the church. Recognizing that we were being given access that many at the time did not have, we did extensive research and consultation with leading theologians and other experts beforehand. I think that the cardinals were surprised by our level of preparation and concern, and we were invited back for many rounds of conversation with them and succeeding heads of dicasteries. There is no better summary of the issues we raised than my beloved friend Kerry Robinson's October 2013 article in *America* magazine, originally entitled "Opening Doors: Women in Dialogue at the Vatican."[1]

In the eleven years since the article's publication, some welcome progress has been made in appointing more women to senior leadership positions in the curia.

1. Kerry Alys Robinson, "I've Been Meeting with Vatican Cardinals about Women in the Church. Here's What Needs to Change," *America*, October 16, 2013, https://www.americamagazine.org/issue/opening-doors.

And yet restoring women to the diaconate and integrating more scriptural readings into the lectionary to feature women as protagonists are among the issues that remain long overdue and utterly frustrating to many of us concerned about the church's health, vitality, and fidelity in its witness to the Good News.

In 2010, Kerry Robinson and I were asked to serve on the Women's Advisory Board of the Woodstock Theological Center at Georgetown. The fellows there felt that women's voices were not sufficiently heard, and they decided to film four of us preaching on the Sunday readings for Advent 2011. Frank and Mary Frost, creators of the documentary *Teilhard: Visionary Scientist*, filmed us in Copley Crypt Chapel on Georgetown's campus, a gorgeous space. Woodstock circulated our preaching to their subscribers on Vimeo, with much positive reception.

A year later, I think with the guidance of the Holy Spirit, I had the idea for a freely accessible, content-controlled website to showcase Catholic women preaching. Diverse in age and ethnicity, women from around the world preach on the lectionary readings for each Sunday and holy day of obligation. We post their five-to-seven-minute video, with a print text, brief bio, and links to the preacher's organizations and publications. We post at least two weeks in advance so that clergy can get homily ideas! These preachings can inspire rich conversation in small Christian communities, in the catechumenate process, and in high school, college, and university classrooms.

I decided to collaborate with colleagues at FutureChurch in Cleveland who, in 2001, had started posting the texts of women's preaching for FutureChurch's annual Mary of Magdala celebrations. Russ Petrus (now

FutureChurch's executive director) designed the website, and we launched Catholic Women Preach in Advent 2016. The website now features over 450 freely accessible homilies. Orbis Books has also published *Catholic Women Preach: Raising Voices, Renewing the Church* in three volumes to feature preachings from the website for each year of the three-year lectionary. The volumes include preaching for each Sunday, holy day of obligation, and several significant women's feast days, with forewords by Barbara Reid, OP, Cecilia González Andrieu, and Mary Catherine Hilkert, OP.

If you go to the website, you will experience the unique, fresh insights that women bring when breaking open the Word. Our preachers are involved in restorative justice and reconciliation. They combat racism, poverty, violence against women and girls, human trafficking, and the climate crisis as they build safe and inclusive communities of mutual care where all are welcome. They demonstrate empathy and compassion as they relate the stories of family, friends, students, fellow parishioners, and community members seeking and sometimes struggling to be credible, joyful, and hope-filled witnesses to the message of Jesus of Nazareth, crucified and risen.

For many women, particularly young Catholic women, Catholic Women Preach instills hope for a Church that might fully recognize, embrace, and deploy their gifts. In the fraught, divided, violent world in which we live, a healthy, transparent, inclusive, vibrant Catholic Church is vital to our future. By allowing laypeople to preach the Word at the Eucharist, the church will take a step in the right direction.

An Experience of Church

Carolyn A. Wright

The truth of God's abundance pulsates in the world. Scripture overflows with stories of a God who creates bountifully, promises countless descendants to Abram, and showers quail and manna upon the weary Israelites.[1] It speaks of a Son who provides gallons of fine wine for wedding guests, feeds four and five thousand "besides women and children," heals innumerable maladies, and dramatically enhances a day's catch by exhausted fishermen with the toss of a net.[2] And, finally, it announces a Spirit who opens the ears of nations, fills fearful hearts with courage, compels a host of believers to carry the mission of Christ forward, and bestows copious charisms and gifts on all the faithful.[3]

We witness the truth of God's abundance in our own lives in the outpouring of water and food for earthquake victims, a fully funded GoFundMe to help a family with outrageous medical bills, golden wheat fields stretching

1. Gen 1:1-31; 15:1-5; Exod 16:4-15.

2. John 2:1-11; Matt 15:29-38; 14:14-21; cf. Luke 17:11-19; 5:1-11.

3. Acts 2:1-13; 2:14-47; 1 Cor 12:1-11, 27-31.

as far as the eye can see, spectacular landscapes worldwide, countless stars in the sky, and the uniqueness of every human person who ever lived. Our God is a God of abundance. Our Scriptures witness this truth. Our own eyes do as well.

As a teenager growing up in a small steel mill town on the Ohio River, summer days provided an abundance of time for riding my bike with friends, visiting the library, playing Wiffle ball with my brothers, swimming in my cousins' pools, churning gallons of ice cream for my grandmother, and fishing for bass. My calendar was full. Yet the summer of 1977 took an unexpected turn that significantly altered my experience of abundance and significantly shaped my experience of church.

My family belonged to St. Bernadette's Catholic Church, a parish of approximately 110 families meeting in a two-story house. The upstairs provided our pastor with a kitchen, living room, guest room, and bedroom. The first floor provided a small entry, a sacristy, and two rooms converted as the nave for worship with a tiny organ, some pews, and steel chairs with kneelers. A small raised extension built with cement block provided the space for an intimate sanctuary. Another two-story building housed our church hall and the pastor's garage. It was more voluminous than the church itself!

Our pastor received word from the diocese in the spring of 1977 that the local Catholic high school needed teachers and hoped to find housing to employ six Dominican sisters. Providentially, the two-story, six-bedroom house next door came up for sale. After many meetings weighing the impact on the parish finances and the mission of our small parish, we discerned that we would take this leap of faith as a community to purchase and renovate this dilapidated house. This was our decision, and each community member needed to contribute.

We were baptized Catholics—older and younger, female and male, single and married, parents and children. We were tradesmen and steelworkers, professionals and railroaders, waitresses and gas attendants, and high school and grade school students. We provided the plumbing, electric, HVAC, carpentry, accounting, sandwich-making, and baking expertise. We labored, debated, prayed, sang, dined, and worshiped together, and that house became a home for six Dominican sisters.

This moment is my first memory of the church as a dynamic, living, contributing reality, a font of God's abundance, and a community set afire. And I must ask, Why are there only a handful of these moments? Why do we shackle and restrain God's abundance, bury it under layers of fear, and live from a place of scarcity instead?[4]

At our lay eucharistic preaching symposium, I once again experienced a faith community setting fear aside for God's abundance. Individually and together, we invested abundant time, talent, and treasure. We were baptized Catholics—older and younger, female and male, single and married, laity, priests, and religious. We were theologians with expertise in liturgy, ecclesiology, canon law, practical theology, ministry, and preaching. We were students and professors. We were facilitators, scholars, practitioners, writers, wordsmiths, and preachers. We hailed from the Philippines, Italy, Germany, Canada, and the United States. We presented substantive and illuminating papers. We listened. We invited and provided responses and critical feedback. We offered insights,

4. Matt 25:14-30.

concerns, and stories through panels and table exchanges. We listened to the Spirit through one another as we labored, debated, prayed, sang, dined, and worshiped together. We followed the beckoning Spirit as we crafted a statement to the Synod on Synodality.

As a practical theologian, I wondered about the experiences of others and wanted to capture firsthand accounts. I distributed the following queries in a survey:

> Considering the following questions, imagine Church in its most ideal realization. Provide a brief description or a few qualities of that ideal realization.
>
> - What three words would you use to describe the symposium?
> - Briefly describe the most salient moment of the symposium and speak about its importance to you.
> - Briefly describe the most salient moment of the symposium for those gathered and speak to its importance.
> - What two or three theological principles were operative during the symposium? How so?
> - How was the symposium an experience of Church for you?[5]

Communally, we imagined church ideally much like the description in the Acts of the Apostles: a gathering of baptized believers of "one heart and soul" in the triune

5. The survey garnered a 96 percent response rate.

God.[6] The Spirit compels us to be about the mission of Jesus Christ in the world. We welcome the "full, conscious, and active" participation called for in liturgical celebrations of the church and the mission of the church.[7] We cooperate with all the charisms the Spirit provides. We are courageous, prophetic, inclusive, compassionate, and merciful.

We described the symposium as a Spirit-filled and Spirit-led event that stirred hope, energy, and engagement. We found the group to be inclusive, kind, and convivial and the labor to be empowering, honest, and joy filled. This faith-filled, thought-provoking, intimate encounter encouraged a communal vision, and overall, the process encouraged thoughtful listening, collaboration, and responsiveness.

Many individuals found the liturgical celebration and the diversity of preachers at services of the Word and the Eucharist to be the most salient moments. Some found the active engagement of the Spirit's many gifts most striking. Many also spoke of the power of listening throughout to the broad horizon of experience. One participant noted, "I think the most salient moment was when we heard from the panelists about their own stories. Some people brought decades of experience and wrestling with lay preaching to our discussion. It reminded me of the importance of our work and how people have felt abandoned by the church for years, if not decades. Yet, they persist and are still hopeful. It was truly inspiring."

6. Acts 4:32-34.

7. Vatican II, *Sacrosanctum Concilium* ("Constitution on the Sacred Liturgy" [SC]) 14.

The most salient communal moments occurred on the last day. We agreed that discerning the convergences, giving voice to an initial synthesis of ideas, calling forth people to draft a preliminary statement for the bishops, promising to provide timely communal feedback, and committing to an orderly dissemination plan were prominent. One participant wrote:

> The most salient moment for us was the morning when we had taken all that we discussed, prayed, and preached about and looked at convergences and what we believed the Spirit was calling us to. Our commitment to sharing this good work far and wide, starting with the Vatican and USCCB offices, became very real when we identified synod participants we knew and would contact, the publications we would send it to, and the networks with whom we would share it. For me, it felt like a Pentecost moment where we were commissioned and compelled to share the good news, believing the work we had been doing would be in service of the Church.

A second participant noted: "Understanding the process and elongated time for implementing a change to Canon Law reframed our dream of being part of the journey, not necessarily the destination. We began to see our call as voicing what is happening in the Church already and challenging the Church to see it and, in some form, regularize it via an amendment to canon 767 §1 and proposing to expand the use of and create new installed ministries."

We realized the moment was not about our preconceived ideas of what we wanted to call the church to but rather about listening, discerning how and to what the

Spirit called us. Our greatest hope was that our labor would be of service to the church and its mission to preach the Good News of Jesus Christ.

Three operative theological foundations surfaced during this gathering. Pneumatology surfaced in the minds of most. We witnessed it as a "Pentecostal moment." "There was a power (of the Spirit) present" and a "sharing of distinct gifts for the common good." We attended to "where the Spirit seemed to be calling us," and "we did all this in the context of prayer, which is the only authentic context in which to listen to the voice of the Spirit."

A second theological principle observed was God's active, ongoing revelation: "The divine encounter to which all the baptized are invited (as *Dei Verbum* states) is continuously mediated not only in scripture and tradition but also through the *sensus fidei*—the developing spiritual insight of the baptized in history. Reading the scripture text and living tradition, we came to new insights into God's call in time for the Church's preaching ministry."

The third operative theological underpinning—providing stability and a call for change—was the nature of the church itself. As one participant voiced: "The Eucharist is, by its very nature, a synodal act. A synodal church seeks out and employs all the gifts for eucharistic preaching that the Holy Spirit has given. One can look at the eucharistic preaching issue from the ordained priest's perspective, configured to Christ. One can also discern the matter from the standpoint of pneumatology and the Church's fundamental call to discern the gifts of the Spirit in every age and circumstance."

The same participant described holding ecclesiology and pneumatology together: "The Church's nature, mission, and ministries cannot be understood apart from a theology of the Holy Spirit. We assume that it is the Church's task in every age to discern the many gifts given for preaching and all the ministries of the Church. Synodality—the way forward is through the practice of synodality—the Church walking together, listening to each other, speaking boldly, and always open to the surprising ways in which the Spirit calls us to mission."

We know God continues to reveal who we are called to be as church: a listening *ecclesia* that, in prayer, attends to the Spirit's beckoning through the *sensus fidei* (all the baptized) and the abundant gifts infused in the church for the mission of Christ in the world.

God's abundance pulsates in the world. Scriptures witness to the truth of it. We witness the truth of it. I experienced it as a woman among theologians, ministers, and preachers who gathered to develop a constructive, theological appeal to the church for lay eucharistic preaching. I experienced it as a girl in a parish community that created a home for Dominican sisters. And I continue to ask, Why are there only a handful of these moments? Why do we shackle and restrain God's abundance, bury it under layers of fear, and, instead, live from scarcity? What might we experience as a synodal church choosing to live from abundance?

Appendix 1

The Code of Canon Law and Preaching[1]

Can. 204 — §1. The Christian faithful are those who, inasmuch as they have been incorporated in Christ through baptism, have been constituted as the people of God. For this reason, made sharers in their own way in Christ's priestly, prophetic, and royal function, they are called to exercise the mission which God has entrusted to the Church to fulfill in the world, in accord with the condition proper to each.

Can. 208 — From their rebirth in Christ, there exists among all the Christian faithful a true equality regarding dignity and action by which they all cooperate in the building up of the Body of Christ according to each one's own condition and function.

Can. 211 — All the Christian faithful have the duty and the right to work so that the divine message of salvation

1. Excerpts from the *Code of Canon Law: Latin-English Edition*, New English Translation, copyright © 2023, Canon Law Society of America, Washington, DC, are reprinted with permission.

more and more reaches all people in every age and in every land.

Can. 225 — §1. Since, like all the Christian faithful, lay persons are designated by God for the apostolate through baptism and confirmation, they are bound by the general obligation and possess the right as individuals, or joined in associations, to work so that the divine message of salvation is made known and accepted by all persons everywhere in the world. This obligation is even more compelling in those circumstances in which only through them can people hear the gospel and know Christ.

Can. 225 — §2. According to each one's own condition, they are also bound by a particular duty to imbue and perfect the order of temporal affairs with the spirit of the gospel and thus to give witness to Christ, especially in carrying out these same affairs and in exercising secular functions.

Can. 756 — §1. With respect to the universal Church, the function of proclaiming the gospel has been entrusted principally to the Roman Pontiff and the college of bishops.

Can. 756 — §2. With respect to the particular church entrusted to him, an individual bishop, who is the moderator of the entire ministry of the word within it, exercises that function; sometimes several bishops fulfill this function jointly with respect to different churches at once, according to the norm of law.

Can. 757 — It is proper for presbyters, who are coworkers of the bishops, to proclaim the gospel of God;

this duty binds especially pastors and others to whom the care of souls is entrusted with respect to the people committed to them. It is also for deacons to serve the people of God in the ministry of the word in communion with the bishop and his presbyterium.

Can. 758 — By virtue of their consecration to God, members of institutes of consecrated life give witness to the gospel in a special way and the bishop appropriately calls upon them as a help in proclaiming the Gospel.

Can. 759 — By virtue of baptism and confirmation, lay members of the Christian faithful are witnesses of the gospel message by word and the example of a Christian life; they can also be called upon to cooperate with the bishop and presbyters in the exercise of the ministry of the word.

Can. 762 — Sacred ministers, among whose principal duties is the proclamation of the gospel of God to all, are to hold the function of preaching in esteem since the people of God are first brought together by the word of the living God, which it is certainly right to require from the mouth of priests.

Can. 763 — Bishops have the right to preach the word of God everywhere, including in churches and oratories of religious institutes of pontifical right, unless the local bishop has expressly forbidden it in particular cases.

Can. 764 — Without prejudice to the prescript of can. 765, presbyters and deacons possess the faculty of preaching everywhere; this faculty is to be exercised with at least the presumed consent of the rector of the church, unless the competent ordinary has restricted or taken away the faculty or particular law requires express permission.

Can. 766 — Lay persons can be permitted to preach in a church or oratory, if necessity requires it in certain circumstances or it seems advantageous in particular cases, according to the prescripts of the conference of bishops and without prejudice to can. 767 §1.

Can. 767 — §1. Among the forms of preaching, the homily, which is part of the liturgy itself and is reserved to a priest or deacon, is preeminent; in the homily the mysteries of faith and the norms of Christian life are to be explained from the sacred text during the course of the liturgical year.

Can. 772 — §1. In the exercise of preaching, moreover, all are to observe the norms issued by the diocesan bishop.

Appendix 2

Essays from *Preaching and the Non-Ordained*

An Interdisciplinary Study[1]

Introduction by Nadine Foley, OP

The period through which the American Churches are passing is one in which more and more Christian people are coming to a mature faith. They seek not a mere passive presence to the rites and ministries of institutional religion but a vital, active participation both in public worship and in the Church's mission to the world. Ours is a personalistic social milieu in which people are conscious of their individual gifts and are motivated to use these gifts appropriately and responsibly. It is a particularly promising time for the Church as a people of God called individually and corporately to become fully alive in the redeeming experience of Jesus Christ.

1. These opening essays from *Preaching and the Non-Ordained: An Interdisciplinary Study*, ed. Nadine Foley (Collegeville, MN: Liturgical Press, 1983) are reprinted with the permission of the publisher. The closing paragraph of each essay has been omitted.

For the Roman Catholic Church, the new self-awareness of its members offers challenge and opportunity. But the consistently recurring question in a number of areas revolves around the issue of whether or not the inherited structures and practices are adaptable to the needs and aspirations of contemporary Catholics and adequate to the task of proclaiming the gospel at what appears to be a critical turning point of human history. One of the questions being raised pertains to preaching, a function currently authorized to be carried out in the liturgical setting by bishops, priests, and deacons. But can preaching be done within the Christian assembly by those who are not ordained? The question goes beyond mere juridical considerations to encompass concerns for the rights of Christians and for the evident charisms that exist among them.

Experience shows that ordination does not infallibly confer the gift of effective preaching. It shows further in many places where non-ordained persons are preaching, that the gift for preaching is widely distributed among the Church's members, and especially among women and men who are actively meeting the many demands of today's ministries.

When thoughtful people reflect upon the situation, it becomes evident that little formal study of the office of preaching, its historical development, and its presumed integral relation to the role of the priest in the celebration of the Eucharist has been done. This fact became particularly evident to American Dominican men and women, members of the Order of Preachers, who have new reasons to assess the meaning of the Order's charism, shared by both its ordained and non-ordained members as they participate in the movements of the present time. Women members of the Order especially have persistent questions about their identity as *preachers* in the light of their own new claims upon full personhood supported both by society and the message of the gospel. It was to address the emerging questions that the Dominican Leadership Conference in 1975 established a special commission to examine and report on issues related to Dominican women and preaching.

That commission[2] first produced a paper, "Unless They Be Sent: A Theological Report on Dominican Women Preaching," for study and reflection by the women's congregations, the provinces of men, and the Dominican laity. Subsequently, a new standing commission was established to continue the exploration. To this group it became clear that the concerns that had motivated their work in a very particular way were shared by many others in the Church in a more general way. The Dominican Leadership Conference then authorized the commission to plan a special conference on preaching by the non-ordained to be developed in an interdisciplinary mode and to be open to all interested persons. This volume contains the papers that formed the core of the discussions held at that event in Columbus, Ohio, October 8-10, 1982.

Opening Remarks by Kathleen Cannon, OP

> *"When the Spirit of truth comes, he will guide you into all the truth; for he will not speak on his own authority, but whatever he hears he will speak, and he will declare*

2. Composed of Dominicans Diana Culbertson, Marie Walter Flood, Dorothy Folliard, Louise Hageman, Thomas O'Meara, and Lucy Vasquez.

> *to you the things that are to come"* (John 16:13 [English Standard Version]).

As Christians, we proclaim our belief in the abiding presence of the Holy Spirit in the community, as immanent to the believing community. The Spirit of Jesus is present, active, living within us. As the heart of the Church, the Spirit is the principle of life and vitality for the community. It is the Spirit who is the source of the prophetic nature of the Christian community. The Spirit guides through human structures and, at least in principle, there is no opposition between the Spirit and the Church, between the Spirit's work and our work. One index of this direction by the Spirit is the gradual arising within the Church of new questions that are resolved through discussion and human exchange, from which the Spirit is not absent. For the Spirit's work, while transcendent, occurs in and through the human experiences of evaluating, trying, testing, asking, studying, discussing.

The matter of this particular conference, namely, preaching by the non-ordained, is one that has come forth within Christian circles. In fact and in spontaneous experience, women and lay men are being asked or "called" to the ministry of preaching, either occasionally or regularly. Further, they are being called even by designated leaders of the Christian community. There are those, too, who have discerned a charism for preaching and who claim that they are able truly to mediate the Gospel of Christ to contemporary Christian communities on the basis their own gospel experience.

On the other hand, the non-ordained are also being denied opportunities to preach. We do not lack for examples, both written and hearsay, of a lay person being directed to speak at a time other than the homily or their words referred to as a "meditation or reflection." At the same time, there are groups within the Church calling for an extension of the situations in which it is permissible for non-ordained persons to preach. Both the Canon Law Society of America and the Dominican Leadership Conference of the United States have been working to this end and have invested time, expertise, and scholarship toward uprooting stubborn residual problems in key areas of the theology of preaching. These are all indicators of rising practical change and mounting theoretical concerns in regard to all forms of the preaching of the gospel by qualified baptized lay persons.

While we are certainly not the first to ask who may preach the Gospel with authority in the midst of the ecclesial assembly, nevertheless there is a certain newness or urgency to the question today. The newness derives from our understanding of the ecclesial nature of the laity, their status as members of God's people and sharers in the salvific mission of the Church. It emerges, too, from the contemporary discussion of the role of women: the existential reality of who women are in general society and therefore in the society of the historical Church is not the same as it has been throughout much of Christian history. Finally, our heightened awareness of the need for evangelization and the new milieu of preaching—the demands that our times place for preaching the Word—underscores the need for a general revitalization of preaching. The questions put to us today call upon us to pay the price of this grace by serious theological reflection carried out in an atmosphere of prayer. This matter, then, is an issue of truly ecclesial concern for all members of the Church—men and women, lay and ordained—for the essential reality before us all is that of preaching the Word of God and how we can best do that in our age.

The matter needs to be faced; to fail to do so would be to fail the challenges inherent in belief. The question arises from faith and demands an answer in faith. It is no Christian solution to bury one's head in the sand. The matter of lay preaching calls for open, honest, theological and ecclesiological reflection and diagnosis to find out what is from the Spirit, to "hold fast what is good, abstain from every form of evil" (1 Thess 5:21-22 [ESV]).

Hence this gathering of learned and committed believers is convened to open up the parameters of the question in an irenic atmosphere. There are multiple facets to the question; we hope to illuminate some. Our intention is to provide some clarity around the issue of ordained/non-ordained preaching from biblical, theological, historical and juridical perspectives. And so the presentations will be concerned with the data of the Scriptures, theological reflection, the Christian tradition, ecclesial law, and liturgy.

Bibliography on Lay Preaching

XVI Ordinary General Assembly of the Synod of Bishops

XVI Ordinary General Assembly of the Synod of Bishops. *Instrumentum Laboris* for the First Session. "For a Synodal Church: Communion, Participation, and Mission." October 2023. https://www.usccb.org/resources/ENG_INSTRUMENTUM-LABORIS.pdf.

XVI Ordinary General Assembly of the Synod of Bishops. *Instrumentum Laboris* for the Second Session. "*How* to Be a Missionary Synodal Church." October 2024. https://press.vatican.va/content/salastampa/en/bollettino/pubblico/2024/07/09/240709d.pdf

XVI Ordinary General Assembly of the Synod of Bishops. Synthesis Report for the First Session. "A Synodal Church in Mission." Vatican City: October 4–29, 2023. https://www.synod.va/content/dam/synod/assembly/synthesis/english/2023.10.28-ENG-Synthesis-Report_IMP.pdf.

Der Synodale Weg. Implementation Text. "Proclamation of the Gospel by Authorised Baptised and Confirmed Persons in Word and Sacrament." March 10, 2023. https://www.synodalerweg.de/fileadmin/Synodalerweg/Dokumente_Reden_Beitraege/beschluesse-broschueren/Englisch/SW-12_Proclamation-of-the-Gospel-by-authorised-baptised-and-confirmed-persons_Implementation-Text.pdf.

General Secretariat of the Synod. XVI Ordinary General Assembly of the Synod of Bishops. "'Enlarge the Space of Your Tent' (Is 54:2): Working Document for the Continental Stage." October 2022. https://www.synod.va/content/dam/synod/common/phases/continental-stage/dcs/Documento-Tappa-Continentale-EN.pdf.

General Secretariat of the Synod. XVI Ordinary General Assembly of the Synod of Bishops. "Towards October 2024." December 11, 2023. https://www.usccb.org/resources/ENG_Document_TOWARDS-OCTOBER-2024_XVI_II-Session.pdf.

United States Conference of Catholic Bishops. "Interim Stage Guidelines." 2024. https://www.usccb.org/resources/Recommendations%20for%20Dioceses%20-%20Interim%20Stage.pdf.

Wooden, Cindy. "Pope Sets up Groups to Study Most Controversial Issues Raised at Synod." Catholic News Service. March 14, 2024. https://www.usccb.org/news/2024/pope-sets-groups-study-most-controversial-issues-raised-synod.

Canon Law, Documents on Ministry, Liturgical Norms, Second Vatican Council

Canon Law Society of America. *Code of Canon Law: Latin-English Edition.* Washington DC: Canon Law Society of America, 1983. https://www.vatican.va/archive/cod-iuris-canonici/cic_index_en.html.

Congregation for Divine Worship. *Directory for Masses with Children.* Washington, DC: United States Catholic Conference, 1974.

Congregation for Divine Worship. *Directory for Sunday Celebrations in the Absence of a Priest.* Washington, DC: United States Catholic Conference, 1988.

Congregation for Divine Worship. *Sunday Celebrations in the Absence of a Priest.* Rev. ed. Washington, DC: USCCB Publishing, 2012.

Congregation for Divine Worship and the Discipline of the Sacraments. *Redemptionis Sacramentum.* "Instruction on Certain Matters to Be Observed or to Be Avoided Regarding the Most Holy Eucharist." March 25, 2004. https://www.vatican.va/roman_curia/congregations/ccdds/documents/rc_con_ccdds_doc_20040423_redemptionis-sacramentum_en.html.

Congregation for the Clergy et al. "Instruction on Certain Questions Regarding the Collaboration of the Non-Ordained Faithful in the Sacred Ministry of Priest" (*Ecclesiae de Mysterio*). August 15, 1997. https://www.vatican.va/roman_curia/pontifical_councils/laity/documents/rc_con_interdic_doc_15081997_en.html.

Coriden, James A., Thomas J. Green, and Donald E. Heintschel, eds. "Decree Implementing Code 766 of the Code of Canon Law." In *The Code of Canon Law: A Text and Commentary*, 550–53. Mahwah, NJ: Paulist Press, 1985.

Doyle, Thomas P. *The Homilist's Guide to Scripture, Theology, and Canon Law.* New York: Pueblo Publishing, 1987.

Fitzgerald, Thomas P., OP. "Canon 766: A Theological Interpretation and Pastoral Application." Thesis for the degree of Master of Theology, Yarra Theological Union, Melbourne, Australia, 1989.

Flannery, Austin, ed. *Vatican Council II: The Basic Sixteen Documents; Constitutions, Decrees, Declarations.* A Completely Revised Translation in Inclusive Language. Collegeville, MN: Liturgical Press, 2014.

Fox, Joseph. "The Homily and the Authentic Interpretation of Canon 767, Art. 1." *Apollinaris* 62 (1989): 123–69.

Francis, Pope. *Antiquum Ministerium.* "Instituting the Ministry of Catechist." Apostolic Letter Issued "Motu Proprio." May 10, 2021. https://www.vatican.va/content

/francesco/en/motu_proprio/documents/papa-francesco-motu-proprio-20210510_antiquum-ministerium.html.

Francis, Pope. "Message on the Fiftieth Anniversary of the Apostolic Letter Issued 'Motu Proprio' *Ministeria Quaedam* of Saint Paul VI." August 15, 2022. https://www.vatican.va/content/francesco/en/messages/pont-messages/2022/documents/20220815-messaggio-ministeria-quaedam.html.

Francis, Pope. *Spiritus Domini.* "Modifying Canon 230 §1 of the Code of Canon Law Regarding Access of Women to the Ministries of Lector and Acolyte." Apostolic Letter Issued "Motu Propio." January 10, 2021. https://www.vatican.va/content/francesco/en/motu_proprio/documents/papa-francesco-motu-proprio-20210110_spiritus-domini.html.

Huels, John M., OSM. "Interpreting an Instruction Approved *in forma specifica.*" *Studia Canonica* 32 (1998): 5–46.

Huels, John M., OSM. "The Law on Lay Preaching: Interpretation and Implementation," 61–79. Presented to the Fifty-Second Annual Convention of the Catholic Law Society of America, Cleveland, OH. Washington DC: Canon Law Society of America, 1990.

Huels, John M., OSM. "Lay Preaching." In *Disputed Questions in the Liturgy Today.* Chicago: Liturgy Training Publications, 1988.

Huels, John M., OSM. *More Disputed Questions on the Liturgy Today.* Chicago: Liturgy Training Publications, 1996.

Huels, John M., OSM. "Sunday Liturgies Without a Priest." *Worship* 64 (1990): 451–60.

John Paul II, Pope. *Christifideles Laici.* "On the Vocation and the Mission of the Lay Faithful in the Church and in the World." Post-Synodal Apostolic Exhortation. December 30, 1988. https://www.vatican.va/content/john-paul-ii/en/apost_exhortations/documents/hf_jp-ii_exh_30121988_christifideles-laici.html.

John Paul II, Pope. *Pastores Dabo Vobis*. "I Will Give You Shepherds." Post-Synodal Apostolic Exhortation. March 25, 1992. https://www.vatican.va/content/john-paul-ii/en/apost_exhortations/documents/hf_jp-ii_exh_25031992_pastores-dabo-vobis.html.

McVann, James. *The Canon Law on Sermon Preaching*. New York: Paulist Press, 1940.

Morrisey, F. G. "Decisions of Episcopal Conferences in Implementing the New Law." *Studia Canonica* 20 (1986): 114–15.

National Conference of Catholic Bishops. "Called and Gifted for the Third Millennium." Washington, DC: USCC, 1995. https://www.usccb.org/committees/laity-marriage-family-life-youth/called-and-gifted-third-millennium-1995.

National Conference of Catholic Bishops' Subcommittee on Lay Ministry. "Lay Ecclesial Ministry: The State of the Questions." Washington DC: USCC, 1999.

National Conference of Catholic Bishops' Subcommittee on Lay Ministry. "Together in God's Service: Toward a Theology of Ecclesial Lay Ministry." Washington DC: USCC, 1998.

Norris, Patrick F., OP. "Lay Preaching and Canon Law: Who May Give a Homily?" *Studia Canonica* 24 (1990): 443–54.

Paul VI, Pope. *Ministeria Quaedam*. "On First Tonsure, Minor Orders, and the Subdiaconate." January 1, 1972. Apostolic Letter given "Motu Proprio." https://www.ewtn.com/catholicism/library/ministeria-quaedam-9006.

Provost, James H. "Brought Together by the Word of the Living God (Canons 762–772)." *Studia Canonica* 23 (1989): 345–71.

Provost, James H. "Canon 766." In *Roman Replies and CLSA Advisory Opinions 1986*. Edited by William A. Schumacher and J. James Cuneo, 71–73. Washington, DC: Canon Law Society of America, 1986.

Rinere, Elissa, CP. "Lay Preaching: By Whose Authority?" *Preach* (May/June 2006): 25–30. https://futurechurch.org/wp-content/uploads/2022/02/Lay-Preaching-By-Whose-Authority-by-Elissa-Rinere-CP.pdf.

Robitaille, Lynda. "An Examination of Various Forms of Preaching: Toward an Understanding of the Homily and Canons 766–767." Address Given at the Annual Meeting of the Canon Law Society of America. St. Louis, October 9, 1996.

Sacred Congregation of the Sacraments. *Immensae Caritatis*. "On Facilitating Reception of Communion in Certain Circumstances." January 29, 1973. https://www.ewtn.com/catholicism/library/on-facilitating-reception-of-communion-in-certain-circumstances-2178.

United States Bishops' Committee on the Laity. "Called and Gifted: The American Catholic Laity." Reflections of the American Bishops Commemorating the Fifteenth Anniversary of the Issuance of the Decree on the Apostolate of the Laity. Washington, DC: USCC, 1980. https://www.usccb.org/resources/called_and_gifted.pdf.

United States Conference of Catholic Bishops. *Co-Workers in the Vineyard of the Lord: A Resource for Guiding the Development of Lay Ecclesial Ministry.* Washington, DC: USCCB Publishing, 2005. https://www.usccb.org/upload/co-workers-vineyard-lay-ecclesial-ministry-2005.pdf.

United States Conference of Catholic Bishops, "Guidelines for Lay Preaching." National Catholic News Service. *Origins* 18, no. 25 (1988): 402–4.

United States Conference of Catholic Bishops. "USCCB Decree Implementing Canon 766 of the Code of Canon Law." USCCB Committee on the Liturgy Newsletter XXXVII (December 13, 2001): 49–50. https://www.usccb.org/beliefs-and-teachings/what-we-believe/canon-law/complementary-norms/canon-766-lay-preaching.

Pastoral Commentary

Baumer, Patricia Hughes. "Empowering a New Voice: The Potential for Lay Preaching." *The Catholic World* (1994): 93–96.

Baumer, Patricia Hughes, and Rev. Tim Power. "Lay Preaching: Babette's Feast for the Church." The National Institute for the Word of God. *The GoodNews Letter* (1997): 1, 4.

Baumer, Patricia Hughes, Trish Sullivan, and Fred Baumer. *Empowered Voices: A Training/Formation Handbook for Homiletic Preaching*. Eden Prairie, MN: Charis Community Publishing, 2024.

Borschel, Audrey. "Excluding Lay Preachers Stifles the Spirit." *National Catholic Reporter* (May 3, 2002).

Cannon, Kathleen, OP. "Opening Remarks." In *Preaching and the Non-Ordained: An Interdisciplinary Study*, edited by Nadine Foley, OP, 7–9. Collegeville, MN: Liturgical Press, 1983.

Carroll, Maureen, and Kathleen Cannon. "Enfleshing the Word: The Case for Lay Preachers." *Liturgy* 24, no. 3 (1979): 174–77.

Castagna, Domingo. "Should the Laity Preach Today?" In *The Renewal of Preaching in Theory and Practice,* edited by Karl Rahner, SJ, 92–98. *Concilium* 33. New York: Paulist Press, 1968.

Center for Applied Research in the Apostolate (CARA). "Getting the Word Out: Lay Preaching in the Diocese of Great Falls-Billings, Montana." *CARA Summary Report* (Summer 2002).

Chopp, Rebecca S. "Proclamation, Women, and the Word." Chapter 1 in *The Power to Speak: Feminism, Language, and God*, 10–39. New York: Crossroad, 1991.

Collins, Mary, OSB. "The Baptismal Roots of the Preaching Ministry." Chapter 10 in *Worship: Renewal to Practice*, 175–95. Washington, DC: Pastoral Press, 1987.

Collins, Mary, OSB. "The Baptismal Roots of the Preaching Ministry." In *Preaching and the Non-Ordained: An Interdisciplinary Study*, edited by Nadine Foley, OP, 111–33. Collegeville, MN: Liturgical Press, 1983.

Delaplane, Joan, OP. "Homily." In *Preaching and the Non-Ordained: An Interdisciplinary Study*, edited by Nadine Foley, OP, 161–65. Collegeville, MN: Liturgical Press, 1983.

Donnelly, Elizabeth, and Russ Petrus, eds. *Catholic Women Preach: Raising Voices, Renewing the Church, Cycle A*. Maryknoll, NY: Orbis Books, 2022.

Donnelly, Elizabeth, and Russ Petrus, eds. *Catholic Women Preach: Raising Voices, Renewing the Church, Cycle B*. Maryknoll, NY: Orbis Books, 2023.

Donnelly, Elizabeth, and Russ Petrus, eds. *Catholic Women Preach: Raising Voices, Renewing the Church, Cycle C*. Maryknoll, NY: Orbis Books, 2024.

Fairbanks, Sarah Ann. "Displaced Persons: Lay Liturgical Preachers at the Eucharist." *Worship* 77, no. 5 (September 2003): 439–57.

Fairbanks, Sarah Ann. "Liturgical Preaching by Lay Ecclesial Ministers: What Difference Does It Make?" *Liturgical Ministry* 15 (Winter 2006): 35–44.

Foley, Nadine, OP. "Introduction." In *Preaching and the Non-Ordained: An Interdisciplinary Study*, edited by Nadine Foley, OP, 3–5. Collegeville, MN: Liturgical Press, 1983.

Heille, Gregory, OP. "Lay Preacher." In *The New Interpreter's Handbook of Preaching*, edited by Paul Scott Wilson, 274–76. Nashville: Abingdon Press, 2008.

Henderson, J. Frank. "The Minister of Liturgical Preaching." *Worship* 56 (1982): 214–30.

Hilkert, Mary Catherine, OP. "Anointed and Sent: The Charism of Preaching." Chapter 4 in *Retrieving Charisms for the Twenty-First Century*, edited by Doris Donnelly, 47–63. Collegeville, MN: Liturgical Press, 1999.

Hilkert, Mary Catherine, OP. "God's Words in Women's Words." *America* (November 27, 1999): 14–18.

Hilkert, Mary Catherine, OP. "The Many Gifts of the Spirit: Lay Preaching and Liturgy." In *The Bible as Word of God*, edited by Diego Irarrázaval and Marie-Theres Wacker, 53–60. *Concilium* 2010, no. 2. London: SCM Press, 2010.

Hilkert, Mary Catherine, OP. "Women and Priestly Ministry: The New Testament Evidence." *Catholic Biblical Quarterly* 41 (October 1979): 608–13.

Hilkert, Mary Catherine, OP. Chapter 9, "Women Preaching the Gospel," and Chapter 10, "The Good News in Different Voices." In *Naming Grace: Preaching and the Sacramental Imagination.* New York: Continuum, 1997.

Hilkert, Mary Catherine, OP. "Women Preaching the Gospel." *Theology Digest* 33, no. 4 (1986): 423–40.

Hill, William J., OP. "Toward a Theology of Preaching: One Model and One Question." In *Preaching and the Non-Ordained: An Interdisciplinary Study*, edited by Nadine Foley, OP, 91–109. Collegeville, MN: Liturgical Press, 1983.

Parachini, Patricia A. *Guide for Lay Preachers.* Chicago: Liturgy Training Publications, 2000.

Parachini, Patricia A., SNJM. *Lay Preaching: State of the Question*. American Essays in Liturgy. Collegeville, MN: Liturgical Press, 1999.

Parachini, Patricia A., and Patrick Lagges. "Charism and Order in Preaching." In *A Handbook for Catholic Preaching*, edited by Edward Foley, Catherine Vincie, and Richard Fragomeni, 264–74. Collegeville, MN: Liturgical Press, 2016.

Provost, James H. "Lay Preaching and Canon Law in a Time of Transition." In *Preaching and the Non-Ordained: An Interdisciplinary Study*, edited by Nadine Foley, OP, 140–58. Collegeville, MN: Liturgical Press, 1983.

Schillebeeckx, Edward, OP. "The Right of Every Christian to Speak in the Light of Evangelical Experience in the Midst of Brothers and Sisters," including responses by Maureen P. Carroll, OP, Donald Goergen, OP, Mary

Catherine Hilkert, OP, and William Skudlarek, OSB. In *Preaching and the Non-Ordained: An Interdisciplinary Study*, edited by Nadine Foley, OP, 11–59. Collegeville, MN: Liturgical Press, 1983.

Schneiders, Sandra, IHM. "New Testament Foundations for Preaching by the Non-Ordained." In *Preaching and the Non-Ordained: An Interdisciplinary Study*, edited by Nadine Foley, OP, 60–90. Collegeville, MN: Liturgical Press, 1983.

Skudlarek, William, OSB. "Assertion without Knowledge? The Lay Preaching Controversy of the High Middle Ages." PhD diss., Princeton University, 1979.

Skudlarek, William, OSB. "Lay Preaching." In *Concise Encyclopedia of Preaching*, edited by William H. Willimon and Richard Lischer, 760–62. Louisville: Westminster John Knox Press, 1995.

Skudlarek, William, OSB. "Lay Preaching and the Liturgy." *Worship* 58 (1984): 500–506.

Wallace, James, CSsR. "Guidelines for Preaching by the Laity: Another Step Backward?" *America* (September 16, 1989): 139–41.

Zikmund, Barbara. "The Struggle for the Right to Preach." In *Women and Religion in America*, edited by Rosemary Radford Ruether and Rosemary Skinner Keller, 193–241. San Francisco: Harper and Row, 1981.

Theology of Ministries and Liturgical Studies

Baldovin, John F. "The Eucharist and Ministerial Leadership." *CTSA Proceedings* 52 (1997): 63–81.

Congar, Yves. "The *Ecclesia* or Christian Community as a Whole Celebrates the Liturgy." In *At the Heart of Christian Worship: Liturgical Essays of Yves Congar*, translated and edited by Paul Philibert, 15–68. Collegeville, MN: Liturgical Press, 2010.

Congar, Yves. *Lay People in the Church: A Study for a Theology of the Laity.* Translated by Donald Attwater. Westminster, MD: Newman Press, 1959.

Fox, Zeni, ed. *Lay Ecclesial Ministry: Pathways Toward the Future.* New York: Rowman and Littlefield, 2010.

Fox, Zeni. *New Ecclesial Ministry: Lay Professionals Serving the Church.* Rev. and exp. ed. Franklin, WI: Sheed & Ward, 2002.

Gaillardetz, Richard R. *Ecclesiology for a Global Church: A People Called and Sent.* Rev. ed. Maryknoll, NY: Orbis Books, 2023.

Gaillardetz, Richard R. "The Theological Reception of Co-Workers in the Vineyard of the Lord." In *Lay Ecclesial Ministry: Pathways Toward the Future*, edited by Zeni Fox, 17–30. New York: Rowman and Littlefield, 2010.

Hahnenberg, Edward P. *Ministries: A Relational Approach.* New York: Crossroad, 2003.

Hahnenberg, Edward. "Theology of Lay Ecclesial Ministry: Future Trajectories." In *Lay Ecclesial Ministry: Pathways Toward the Future*, edited by Zeni Fox, 67–83. New York: Rowman and Littlefield, 2010.

Heille, Gregory, OP. "Preaching in the Roman Catholic Theological Family." In *Preaching the Manifold Grace of God: Theologies of Preaching in Historical Theological Families*, vol. 1, edited by Ronald J. Allen, 27–52. Eugene, OR: Wipf & Stock, 2022.

Legrand, Hervé-Marie. "The Presidency of the Eucharist According to the Ancient Tradition." In *Living Bread, Saving Cup*, edited by R. Kevin Seasoltz, 196–221. Collegeville, MN: Liturgical Press, 1982.

Luciani, Rafael. *Synodality: A New Way of Proceeding in the Church*: Translated by Joseph Owens, SJ. New York: Paulist Press, 2022.

Madar, Martin. *The Church of God and Its Human Face: The Contribution of Joseph A. Komonchak to Ecclesiology.* Eugene, OR: Wipf & Stock, 2019.

McCord, H. Richard Jr. "Co-Workers in the Vineyard of the Lord: A Pastoral Perspective on Its Reception." In *Lay Ecclesial Ministry: Pathways Toward the Future*, edited by Zeni Fox, 3–15. New York: Rowman and Littlefield, 2010.

Nutt, Maurice J., CSsR. *Deep Down in My Soul: An African American Catholic Theology of Preaching*. Maryknoll, NY: Orbis Books, 2023.

O'Meara, Thomas F., OP. *Theology of Ministry*. Completely rev. ed. New York: Paulist Press, 1999.

Osborne, Kenan B. *Ministry: Lay Ministry in the Roman Catholic Church; Its History and Theology*. New York: Paulist Press, 1993.

Philibert, Paul, OP. *The Priesthood of the Faithful: Key to a Living Church*. Collegeville, MN: Liturgical Press, 2005.

Power, David N. *Gifts That Differ: Lay Ministries Established and Unestablished*. Studies in the Reformed Rites of the Catholic Church 8. New York: Pueblo Publishing, 1985.

Schillebeeckx, Edward. *The Church with a Human Face: A New and Expanded Theology of Ministry*. Translated by John Bowden. New York: Crossroad, 1985.

Wood, Susan K., ed. *Ordering the Baptismal Priesthood: Theologies of Lay and Ordained Ministry*. Collegeville, MN: Liturgical Press, 2003.

Symposium Participants

"The Pastoral Charge for Lay Catholic Eucharistic Preaching"

A Homiletic and Theological Symposium
March 11 to 14, 2024
Aquinas Institute of Theology,
St. Louis, Missouri

Participants

1. Maxime Allard, OP, PhD, Dominicans of Canada and Professor of Philosophy, Dominican University College, Ottawa
2. Kayla August, MPS, Boston College PhD student in Theology and Education (Preaching), School of Theology and Ministry at Boston College
3. Kerstin-Marie Berretz, OP, Dipl. Theol., *Arenberger Dominikanerinnen*, *Institut für Pastoralhomiletik* Board of Directors, DMin in Preaching student at Aquinas Institute of Theology, and High School Theology Teacher, *Kolleg St. Thomas*, Vechta, Germany
4. Mary Erika Bolaños, PhD, Principal of the UST Senior High School, Associate Professor of Theology at the Institute of Religion of the University of Santo Tomas, Manila,

and the Institute of Preaching of the Philippine Dominican Center for Institutional Studies, Quezon City, and Institute of Preaching Lay Missionary Preacher

5. Wayne Cavalier, OP, PhD, Director, Congar Institute for Ministry Development, and Associate Professor of Theology and DMin Director, Oblate School of Theology, San Antonio
6. Nathan P. Chase, PhD, Assistant Professor of Liturgical and Sacramental Theology, Aquinas Institute of Theology
7. Elizabeth A. Donnelly, MTS, Co-founder and Preacher Coordinator, Catholic Women Preach
8. Megan Effron, MDiv, PhD Student in Systematic Theology, University of Notre Dame
9. Tom Esselman, CM, PhD, Assistant Provincial Superior, Congregation of the Mission, The Vincentians Western Province, St. Louis
10. Sara Fairbanks, OP, PhD, Adrian (Michigan) Dominican Sisters and Associate Professor of Theology and Preaching, Aquinas Institute of Theology
11. Ann Garrido, DMin, Associate Professor of Homiletics, Aquinas Institute of Theology, and Consultant with Triad Consulting Group
12. Edward P. Hahnenberg, PhD, Breen Chair in Catholic Theology, John Carroll University, Cleveland
13. Gregory Heille, OP, DMin, Dominican Central Province of St. Albert the Great and Professor of Preaching and Evangelization, Director of Doctor of Ministry in Preaching, and Codirector of Delaplane Preaching Initiative, Aquinas Institute of Theology
14. Ruth Anne Henderson, OP, MA, past president of the European Council of Lay Dominican Fraternities, Turin
15. Mary Catherine Hilkert, OP, PhD, Dominican Sisters of Peace and Professor of Theology, University of Notre Dame
16. Layla A. Karst, PhD, Assistant Professor of Theological Studies, Loyola Marymount University

17. Martin Madar, PhD, Associate Professor of Theology, Xavier University, Cincinnati
18. Megan McElroy, OP, DMin, Leadership Team, Dominican Sisters ~ Grand Rapids, and Doctor of Ministry in Preaching, Aquinas Institute of Theology
19. Maurice J. Nutt, CSsR, DMin, Redemptorist Missionary Preacher, Denver Province, and Adjunct Professor of Preaching and Evangelization and New Frontiers in African American Preaching Consultant, Aquinas Institute of Theology
20. F. Javier Orozco, OFS, PhD, Executive Director of Human Dignity and Intercultural Affairs, Archdiocese of St. Louis, and New Frontiers in Preaching Academy Consultant, Aquinas Institute of Theology
21. Barbara E. Reid, OP, PhD, Dominican Sisters ~ Grand Rapids, President and Carroll Stuhlmueller Distinguished Professor of New Testament Studies at Catholic Theological Union
22. Theresa Rickard, OP, DMin, Dominican Sisters of Blauvelt Leadership Team and past president of RENEW International
23. Elissa Rinere, CP, JCD, Sisters of the Cross and Passion, Canonical Consultant
24. Casey Stanton, MDiv, Co-director of Discerning Deacons
25. Mark Wedig, OP, PhD, Southern Dominican Province of St. Martin de Porres, President and Professor of Liturgical Theology, Aquinas Institute of Theology
26. Deborah Wilhelm, DMin, Adjunct Professor of Preaching and Evangelization and Codirector of Delaplane Preaching Initiative, Aquinas Institute of Theology
27. Carolyn A. Wright, DMin, Assistant Professor of Pastoral Theology, Director of Theological Field Education, Aquinas Institute of Theology

Advance Praise for *Saving Lily*

"Well done. Easy to read and the truth about addiction."

—Marilyn Kirkpatrick, Clark County Commissioner and former Legislator

"This book was a hard read and an easy read. Hard because it covers the truth about how the disease of addiction works and what it will take to provide treatment to all. Easy because Marlon and Kantor weave together gripping true experiences with an academic understanding of the disease and treatment, making it an interesting read for both expert and layman."

—Shelley Berkley, Las Vegas Mayor and former US Congresswoman

"A groundbreaking contribution to addiction literature, *Saving Lily* merges raw memoir with clinical expertise to redefine crisis narratives. Marlon and Kantor deliver electrifying urgency through two powerful perspectives: a clinician's transformative journey and a resilient woman's decades-long battle against co-occurring disorders. Their visionary analysis of systemic healthcare failures and advocacy for integrated recovery models charts essential pathways through our opioid crisis. This definitive work stands as an indispensable compass for policymakers, clinicians, and communities seeking transformative solutions."

—Frank-Jürgen Richter, Chairman and Founder, Horasis, Switzerland

"This is more than a recovery story—it's a reckoning with the systems that fail so many. *Saving Lily* is raw, rigorous, and relentlessly human. Dr. David Marlon doesn't just tell the story of recovery—he shows us what it costs, what it demands, and what it means to fight for someone else's life as if it were your own. Through lived experience, clinical clarity, and real-world practice, he offers a clear view of what effective, person-centered care can look like—and what must shift across systems to make it sustainable, accessible, and real. I recognize the truth in these pages—it's both a testimony and a blueprint. This unflinching narrative doesn't just critique what's broken—it calls us to build life bridges rooted in respect, compassion, and dignity. *Saving Lily* pressed on my heart and my calling. Every chapter demanded attention—from both the advocate and the human in me."

—Nyla Christian, Executive Director, Center for African American Recovery Development, National Recovery Advocate & Strategist

"*Saving Lily* is a powerful, unflinching, and deeply compassionate guide to understanding and treating the deadly brain disease of addiction. Dr. Dave Marlon weaves his own harrowing journey with the story of Lily. A woman whose battle with co-occurring disorders and homelessness lays bare the urgency of integrated, dignified, and person-centered care. What results is more than a book, it is a manual, a mirror, and a mission. Both clinically sound and emotionally searing, this work belongs in the hands of every mental health professional, faith leader, and advocate committed to healing our most wounded neighbors. As a clinician, priest, and someone who shares in Dr. Marlon's mission through our work at Vegas Stronger and beyond, I can attest to the wisdom, clarity, and heart this book offers. Dave has not only written a blueprint for recovery, he's modeled a life of purpose, transformation, and service. *Saving Lily* is a gift to the field, to the community, and to the soul. It reminds us that no one is too far gone, and that healing is not only possible, it's holy."

—Rev. Nicholas L. Neubauer, LCSW

"Real talk from the front lines: Kantor and Marlon take on addiction and co-occurring disorders with empathy, rigor, and years of fieldwork. They trace the human toll and map the systemic repairs we actually need, and how they work in the real-world, not just in theory. This book is a must-read for anyone looking to bridge the gap between idealism and realism when it comes to addiction and recovery."

—Cynthia Johnson, Entrepreneur, Author of *Platform: The Art and Science of Personal Branding*